The Eighteenth Century:
A World History

T0399254

鈴木春信画

The New Oxford World History

The Eighteenth Century: A World History

By John O. Voll

OXFORD
UNIVERSITY PRESS

OXFORD
UNIVERSITY PRESS

Oxford University Press is a department of the University of Oxford.
It furthers the University's objective of excellence in research, scholarship,
and education by publishing worldwide. Oxford is a registered trade mark of
Oxford University Press in the UK and in certain other countries.

Published in the United States of America by Oxford University Press
198 Madison Avenue, New York, NY 10016, United States of America.

© Oxford University Press 2025

CIP data is on file at the Library of Congress.

ISBN 9780195153187 (hbk.)
ISBN 9780195338003 (pbk.)

Printed by Integrated Books International, United States of America

*Frontispiece: "Chatsumi" (gathering tea leaves), Japanese woodcut print by
Harunobu Suzuki, ca. 1750–70.* Library of Congress Prints and Photographs Division

Contents

Editors' Preface

This book is part of the New Oxford World History, an innovative series that offers readers an informed, lively, and up-to-date history of the world and its people that represents a significant change from the "old" world history. Only a few years ago, world history generally amounted to a history of the West—Europe and the United States—with small amounts of information from the rest of the world. Some versions of the old world history drew attention to every part of the world *except* Europe and the United States. Readers of that kind of world history could get the impression that somehow the rest of the world was made up of exotic people who had strange customs and spoke difficult languages. Still another kind of "old" world history presented the story of areas or peoples of the world by focusing primarily on the achievements of great civilizations. One learned of great buildings, influential world religions, and mighty rulers but little of ordinary people or more general economic and social patterns. Interactions among the world's peoples were often told from only one perspective.

This series tells world history differently. First, it is comprehensive, covering all countries and regions of the world and investigating the total human experience—even those of so-called "peoples without histories" living far from the great civilizations. "New" world historians thus share in common an interest in all of human history, even going back millions of years before there were written human records. A few "new" world histories even extend their focus to the entire universe, a "big history" perspective that dramatically shifts the beginning of the story back to the Big Bang. Some see the "new" global framework of world history today as viewing the world from the vantage point of the moon, as one scholar put it. We agree. But we also want to take a close-up view, analyzing and reconstructing the significant experiences of all of humanity.

This is not to say that everything that has happened everywhere and in all time periods can be recovered or is worth knowing, but that there is much to be gained by considering both the separate and interrelated stories of different societies and cultures. Making these connections is still another crucial ingredient of the "new" world history. It emphasizes connectedness and interactions of all kinds—cultural, economic, political, religious, and social—involving peoples, places, and processes. It makes comparisons and finds similarities. Emphasizing both the comparisons and interactions is critical to developing a global framework that can deepen and broaden historical understanding, whether the focus is on a specific country or region or on the whole world.

The rise of the new world history as a discipline comes at an opportune time. The interest in world history in schools and among the general public is vast. We travel to one another's nations, converse and work with people around the world, and are changed by global events. War and peace affect populations worldwide as do economic conditions and the state of our environment, communications, and health and medicine. The New Oxford World History presents local histories in a global context and gives an overview of world events seen through the eyes of ordinary people. This combination of the local and the global further defines the new world history. Understanding the workings of global and local conditions in the past gives us tools for examining our own world and for envisioning the interconnected future that is in the making.

Bonnie G. Smith
Anand Yang

CHAPTER I

The World of 1700
Continuity and Change

At the beginning of the eighteenth century, the Kangxi emperor of China welcomed Jesuits from Europe to his court. A Jesuit missionary reported that he was "desirous of being instructed in the European sciences" and had daily tutorials.[1] One of his Jesuit instructors in astronomy, Ferdinand Verbiest, recalled that when he came to the court, "I was always immediately admitted to the private rooms of the Emperor. . . . With such a burning desire, indeed, was the Emperor carried away by astronomical affairs!!"[2] Jesuits had worked with Chinese emperors for almost a century at the beginning of Kangxi's long reign (1661–1722). They were trusted and influential advisors both in diplomatic and scientific affairs and their contributions to Chinese intellectual and economic life were welcomed.

A century later, other Europeans faced the Qianlong emperor, who had quite different attitudes. Lord George Macartney, a politically influential peer who had been a British imperial administrator in the Caribbean and India, led a mission to negotiate trade agreements with China. At the end of the discussions, the Qianlong emperor wrote to King George III of Great Britain, telling him in 1793 that "we have never valued ingenious articles, nor do we have the slightest need of your country's manufactures."[3] This response did not signify a withdrawal of China from the world but rather, it shows a lack of awareness of the changing nature of global affairs.

The Kangxi emperor and the Jesuits had much in common and lived in a world in which the economic and political power of the major societies was quite evenly balanced. The world of the Qianlong emperor and Macartney, at the end of the eighteenth century, was beginning to experience the great divergences among world societies characteristic of the nineteenth-century modern world.

The Kangxi emperor ruled a dynamically expanding domain that was among the most powerful in the world. He was the second emperor in the Qing dynasty, which was established by the Manchu conquest of

The Chinese emperor Kangxi went on inspections tours like the one shown in this painting in the southern provinces to emphasize the power of the new Qing dynasty. The empire expanded significantly during his reign and inspection tours confirmed control by the central government. © RMN-Grand Palais/Art Resource, NY

China in the middle of the seventeenth century. He successfully completed the conquest and established stable rule during his sixty-one-year reign. The Manchus came from the lands north of China, and Kangxi worked to create a cosmopolitan imperial court in which Manchu and Chinese officials could work together effectively. In this context, he welcomed the exchange of scientific ideas among the Chinese and Jesuit scholars in his court.

At the beginning of the eighteenth century, power and wealth were roughly balanced among the major regions of the world. By the early nineteenth century, the Chinese emperors were dealing with a new form of political organization, the emerging European imperial nation-states, and the beginnings of Western European industrial societies. The earlier rough balance of power was beginning to be upset. These changes were not just a natural historical ebb and flow of power. They proved to be major transformations in economic, social, and political life around the world that were becoming part of global life.

People in many places knew that they were living in an age of change, but the changes took unexpected, and possibly inconceivable, forms. At the beginning of the century, Mary Morgan Pennell, a Quaker minister in Pennsylvania, lived in one of the newer urban-agricultural societies in the world, a British colony in North America. She had come to Pennsylvania from Wales in 1694. When she became a minister she "spoke of a trying day she had seen coming on this Nation, advising all to prepare for it."[4]

Pennell immigrated to Pennsylvania as a part of the development of the new Quaker society on the frontier of European North America. The Quaker movement (the Society of Friends) arose in the religious turmoil of the English Civil War in the mid-seventeenth century. Pennell's views illustrate the Quaker expectations that they were living in the "trying day" at the end of the world. She believed she was living in a world that had been defined by a major seventeenth-century Quaker leader, George Fox. The establishment of the Quaker community in the wilderness frontier of North America resonated with Fox's tale of how "the true Church fled into the wilderness" in preparation for a great coming struggle. Based on the imagery of the biblical book of Revelation he announced his participation in the apocalyptic War of the Lamb, which would begin with the return of Jesus, the Lamb of God. Fox proclaimed that "the Lamb and the Saints shall have the victory. . . . The joyful days are coming."[5]

Pennell's community did experience major changes, but the transformations that her Quaker piety predicted were dramatically different from the actual changes during the following century. The wars in North America during the eighteenth century were not the trying days of the end of the world, and an independent United States with steamships docked in Philadelphia was not part of the vision of the coming joyful days of Fox's prophecies.

While the religious world of Pennell was dramatically changing along with the political world of the Kangxi emperor, the world of global trade and commerce was also changing. In 1700 Mulla Abdul Ghafur, perhaps the most powerful merchant and ship-owner in the seaport of Surat, in India, could become wealthy exporting cotton cloth. This cloth was produced by a large network of independent weavers whose products Ghafur purchased through brokers. Although this process was not a factory system, it produced large amounts of cloth for export. He began as a poor peddler but became very rich through aggressive participation in the Red Sea trade. It was reported by a Scottish merchant adventurer who knew him that he "drove a Trade equal to the *English East-india Company*,"[6] one of the largest global trading companies of the time. A problem that he faced was the growth of piracy by some Europeans in the western Indian Ocean, and he profited by mobilizing other Muslim merchants to protect Muslim pilgrims on ships going to Mecca in the Red Sea region. Eventually, as the European trading companies emerged as major international economic powers, independent merchants like Mulla Abdul Ghafur lost their local dominance, but in 1700 the shift in power was not yet visible.[7]

Indian cotton became a favorite cloth among people in Western Europe and many other regions in the world, including West Africa, where it was an important exchange product in the emerging slave trade. Because of its high quality and low cost, Indian cotton dominated the rapidly expanding global market. In Britain, for example, Daniel Defoe, a woolen cloth merchant as well as the author of the novel *Robinson Crusoe*, wrote that "the Wearing and Using Printed or Painted Callicoes [imported from India] as they are now almost universally worn and used in Great Britain, is ruinous to or inconsistent with the Prosperity of our English Manufacturers, as well those of Wool as those of silk" and recommended "the total prohibiting of the Wearing and Using of Printed or Painted Callicoes in Great Britain."[8] There was little expectation that these conditions would change, so Great Britain, for example, was forced to impose import restrictions to protect its own, less-efficient textile industries.

A century later, the Indian cotton industry was becoming a marginal part of the world textile market. At the beginning of the century neither the Indian producer nor the English consumer would have expected this transformation. The change was more than simply an alteration of market share. A new mode of production of cloth in factories using newly invented machinery like the cotton gin was developed in England and the world market came to be dominated by the products of the mills of Lancashire, England. The development of the cotton mills was part of the Industrial Revolution that began in Western Europe in the eighteenth century. The Industrial Revolution transformed the world cotton industry as it was beginning to transform most of the rest of human life.

The lives of the Kangxi emperor, Mary Pennell, and Mulla Abdul Ghafur reflect important political, religious, and economic dimensions of the world at the beginning of the eighteenth century. Their world is one of staggering diversity. Small hunting and gathering bands, large nomadic tribes, agricultural villages, and huge urban imperial systems all coexisted. During the eighteenth century, all of these ways of life and social organization experienced major transformations, while at the same time maintaining significant continuity with the past.

This context of continuity and change gives world history in the eighteenth century a special character. The historical experiences of this

Indian cotton cloth, whether embroidered as in this wall hanging or printed with popular patterns, dominated the global textile markets in the early eighteenth century. Indian competition forced the British producers to adopt Indian decorative styles and to develop new production technologies, which became central to the Industrial Revolution. Eileen Tweedy/The Art Archive at Art Resource, NY century are inevitably viewed through the lens of what came later. By the nineteenth century, world history is the history of the "modern" world, and the eighteenth century is sometimes described as part of "early modern" history. However, peoples and societies in the eighteenth century are *not* modern, if one defines a modern society as an industrial, primarily urban, society operating in the political context of nation-states. Similarly, the history of the eighteenth-century world is sometimes seen as the final era of "pre-modern" history. However, societies in the eighteenth century are not simple continuations of medieval, classical, or older tribal forms of human association. Neither medieval nor modern, the world of the eighteenth century is both a time of significant transformation of global and local patterns from "pre-modern" to "modern," and an era whose ways of life and social organization have their own distinctive character.

A world traveler in 1700 would see many things that had existed for millennia. The landscape of large societies was dominated by agricultural villages, since the overwhelming majority of humans lived in rural areas and directly engaged in food production. In rural France, as elsewhere, agriculture, in the words of a 1698 report of a central government administrator, "seems to have been in its present state since a very ancient age."[9] Scattered throughout the agricultural areas were centrally and strategically located cities that were centers of political control and economic distribution. The major large civilizations in China, South Asia, the Middle East, and Europe were urban-dominated agricultural societies, with cities controlling peasant farming populations.

Agricultural societies without major cities were still important in 1700 in some parts of the world, including Central Africa and the Great Plains of North America, but their continued independent existence was challenged by the expansion of the major urban-based societies. Nomadic peoples controlled open regions around these larger urban-agricultural societies and had, in previous times, the capacity to organize large chieftaincies with the power to conquer the more settled areas. The great Mongol Empire of the twelfth and thirteenth centuries and the Manchu conquest of China illustrate the effectiveness of these non-urban groups. Elsewhere smaller ethnically distinctive societies led by chieftains maintained separate existences in relatively isolated places like the islands of the South Pacific.

In societies around the world in 1700, the basic sources of energy were the renewable resources of sunlight, wind, and moving water and animal and human power. The most important activity, in which most of the world's people were directly involved, was the production of food. The methods they used had been modified over the centuries but remained basically the same as those of early farmers.

The greatest changes over the centuries came in the methods of organization and control of activities of large numbers of people. Clans and chieftaincies of the earliest human societies had, in some places, become city-states in the beginnings of ancient civilizations. The city-states, in turn, become large empires—centralized political systems ruling diverse peoples. These city-based states and empires were the political core of the large urban agricultural civilizations. By the beginning of the eighteenth century, most humans, whether city-dwellers or agricultural villagers, lived within the territories of the urban agricultural civilizations. The Qing dynasty of Kangxi, for example, controlled the densely populated areas of central China, and the dynasty's expansion policies brought previously independent agriculturalists under imperial control. The cities of the ancient and medieval worlds were similar to the cities that the traveler in 1700 would have visited.

In economic life, the scale of trade among peoples had grown significantly over the centuries. By 1700, the whole world was part of a collection of trading networks that exchanged products from North and South America, Eurasia, and Africa. This expanded scope for interaction had a major impact on the way people lived. Products such as coffee, tea, maize, and chocolate were changing the daily lives of many people. In general, consumer goods became more important than luxury goods in global trade, as a part of a long-term trend. However, the products traded were still the regular products of farmers and artisans in urban agricultural societies rather than manufactured goods from an industrial society. Coffee, tea, maize, and other goods were not new. What was new was their global availability.

During the following century, significant changes created the foundations for a new type of society and new modes of production. The world traveler at the beginning of the nineteenth century could see a different world emerging. In 1814 the romantic poet William Wordsworth already saw the disappearance of the open "wilderness" and the transformation of the agricultural village into the industrial city: "From the germ / Of some poor hamlet, rapidly produced / Here a huge town, continuous and compact / Hiding the face of earth for leagues /. . . . And, wheresoe'er the traveler turns his steps / He sees the barren wilderness erased, or disappearing."[10] Richard Guest, a chronicler of the development of cotton manufacturing in England, observed in 1823 that the "curiosity of the traveler" would be excited by the "vast brick edifices in the vicinity of all the great manufacturing towns in the south of Lancashire, towering to the height of seventy or eighty feet" where it was possible to perform the work that had formerly employed whole villages.[11] The new landscape was shaped by the emerging industrial cities and factory towns, while the old farming villages and pre-industrial cities, with their roots in antiquity, were being transformed and replaced.

By 1800 modern industrial society was beginning to emerge in Western Europe. This new type of society was dominated by large cities that were centers of industrial production. Modern political systems were more territorial and "nation-based," with the model image being the sovereign, territorial nation-state. In intellectual and ideological terms, the millennia-old traditions of religious faith were being reconceived or replaced by more secularist and rationalist worldviews.

The transformations involved a growing role for European states and economies in world affairs. The Kangxi emperor's descendants lost wars to European powers just as the Indian cotton merchants lost markets to the new British textile industry and the frontier societies like Pennsylvania displaced existing herding and agricultural communities. During the nineteenth century, European products came to dominate global markets in the same way that European military forces conquered much of the world. The emerging history of "the modern" is dominated by European, and more broadly, Western societies.

Historians argue about how the West, meaning the states and societies of Western Europe and North America, came to such a position of global dominance. Some say that the dominance of the West was somehow inevitable. In this view, even though Western Europe was weak and marginal throughout much of world history, it had special characteristics that created the basis for the emergence of the modern industrial society that came to dominate the world by the end of the nineteenth century. The heritage of Greek rationalism or the special role of merchants in medieval European societies or the incentive given to the development of capitalism by Protestant attitudes toward work are among the many factors that different scholars have described as being sources of the West's special character. Others argue that Europe is not exceptional—its history is a part of the broader pattern of world history. In this perspective, specific developments shaped the "rise of the West," but the West's global domination was not inevitable. China was as prosperous and as well developed in the early modern era as Western Europe, and may, in fact, have had greater wealth. However, it was in Western Europe, and not in China or India, that the old patterns of urban-agricultural societies were transcended and the new industrial society emerged. This process of transformation forms an important part of the history of the world in the eighteenth century.

A discussion between the king of Sweden and the grand vizier of the Ottoman Empire in 1711 illustrates important ways that states interacted at the beginning of the eighteenth century. Charles XII, the king of Sweden, had a cup of coffee with grand vizier Baltaji Mehmed Pasha, the highest-ranking administrator of the Ottoman (Turkish) Empire, on the banks of the Prut River in 1711 in present-day Moldova. The Ottoman army of the grand vizier had just defeated the Russian army led by Peter the Great, the powerful reforming czar of an expanding Russian Empire, while King Charles had just lost a major war to the Russians and was seeking Ottoman help. King Charles was angry because the grand vizier had given favorable terms of surrender to the czar. The king's ambassador, Count Stanislaw Poniatowski, reported the event, noting that the king asked the grand vizier "if he was not responsible to his Master for having neglected to make use of his Advantage." The vizier replied that "having thought proper to make a peace so advantageous and honourable, the Grand Signior [the Sultan] would intirely approve of it." The count noted, "While they were talking, Coffee was brought in, and the King drank one dish."[12]

The conversation over coffee helped to shape the structure of power and diplomacy in central and eastern Europe. The Ottoman willingness to let the Russian army withdraw essentially intact allowed Russia to expand its influence in northern Europe, and it confirmed the decline of Sweden's position as a major military power. This, in turn, influenced outcomes of wars in central and western Europe that were defining the emerging unstable balance of power in the continent. The situation in which the king of Sweden and the grand vizier had their coffee reflects the relative equality in terms of power of the larger states and societies in the early eighteenth century. Russia, Sweden, and the Ottoman Empire were structurally quite similar in terms of military power. As they demonstrated in the wars at the beginning of the century, each had the capacity to defeat the other in battle, depending upon local conditions rather than qualitative differences in technology. There was not yet a divide between "industrial" and "developing" societies nor a conscious definition of the "West" as distinct and separate from some vaguely defined "East."

While Ottoman, Russian, and Swedish societies were different in terms of specifics of language, religion, and culture, they were basically similar in terms of the economic base of society and the general view of the world of the rulers and people. Economic productivity was built on pre-industrial technologies and the political legitimacy of the rulers was believed to have religious foundations. The leaders could understand each other even as they fought and negotiated.

Negotiations between Roman Catholic popes and the Kangxi emperor at the beginning of the eighteenth century were similar. The Jesuits in the Chinese imperial court incorporated traditional Confucian rites into their church services. In what has come to be called the Rites Controversy in Roman Catholic history, this accommodation was controversial, and criticized by Pope Clement XI, who later banned it. During the Easter season in 1700, Jesuits denied the Chinese who had converted to Christianity confession and communion, citing Pope Clement's position. A report by the papal ambassador to the Chinese court, Cardinal Tournon, says that a large group of protesters attacked the local bishop and that they "declared aloud, that they would renounce Christianity, and go directly to Hell it self", rather than confess to any but the Jesuits.[13] Christian and Confucian traditions were different, but believers in the traditions could understand each other religiously in important ways. Like the Swedish king and the grand vizier, the emperor and the pope still both lived in historic urban agricultural societies. This was not an early phase of a conflict between modern-Western and local traditions.

While the historic cultures of the great urban agricultural societies were different, new products such as chocolate, coffee, and tea were changing habits of domestic and public life across the boundaries of tradition. A French lady, Madame d'Aulnoy, traveling in the Iberian Peninsula in the early eighteenth century, could describe in her letters the provisions brought daily to the king of Portugal's house: "There is distributed both tame and wild Fowl, Fish, Chocolate, Fruit, Ice, Charcoal, Wax-Candles, Oyl, Bread, and in a word, everything that is necessary for Life."[14] Similarly, in a novel about a French nobleman who brought his family to Constantinople (Istanbul) in 1702, Penelope Aubin tells a tale of his daughter's life as a prisoner in a Turkish palace. As the daughter and her maid plan their escape, they "thank'd the Eunuchs who had brought in Chocolate for their Breakfast."[15] Chocolate may not have been "necessary for Life" among the common people, but by the beginning of the eighteenth century, this relatively new product from the Western Hemisphere had become a normal part of domestic life in Western Europe and Turkey and other places around the globe.

The trade in these products involved global networks of exchange. In coffee, for example, a Scottish adventurer who spent his time in the

This Ottoman courtier is carrying a cup of coffee. Both the coffee, which is probably from Yemen, and the Chinese porcelain cup were important products in the expanding global markets for consumer goods in the eighteenth century. Gianni Dagli Orti/ The Art Archive at Art Resource, NY

East Indies from 1688 to 1723, "trading and travelling by sea and land," described Betlefackee (Bayt al-Faqih) in Yemen as "the greatest Market for Coffee in the World. It supplies *India, Persia, Turkey* in *Asia, Africa* and *Europe*, besides *England, France* and *Holland* with Coffee-beans."[16]

When the Swedish king and the grand vizier had their coffee and conversation, Western Europeans had only recently been introduced to the drink. An Ottoman ambassador introduced coffee to the French court in 1669 and it rapidly became a popular drink among the elite of Western Europe. The first coffeehouse in Paris was established in 1689, and they soon became numerous. Montesquieu, in his *Persian Letters*, has his fictional Persian visitor to France report in 1713, "Coffee is very much used at Paris; here are a great many public houses where they sell it."[17] Methods and products like coffee, chocolate, and tea, which had been novelties in the seventeenth century, were becoming important regular parts of social, economic, and political life.

The leaders involved in the battle on the Prut in 1711 and the subsequent conversation over coffee lived in a distinctive world. Charles XII, Peter the Great, and Grand Vizier Baltaji Mehmed Pasha each represented a different cultural tradition. The Sweden of King Charles was identified with the major Western European developments of the seventeenth century, while Peter the Great was working to transform a society built on foundations of Eastern Orthodox Christianity, and the grand vizier administered the largest empire in the Muslim world. Yet despite their differences, there were fundamental similarities. None of the three civilizations was industrial or modern. None of the civilizations was in a position to impose its culture on other civilizations, but each was active in adapting elements from other civilizations for use within their own societies. Sometimes this involved self-conscious acts of imitation, like the military reforms of Peter the Great, who hired experts from the West to create a European-style army. At other times, this interaction of cultures was the product of popular tastes, as in the popularity of Indian cloth in Western Europe. Part of the distinctiveness of this world was the growing intensity of interaction among societies and peoples and the relative balance of cultural power—which meant that no one civilization was dominant. It was an era of competitive alternatives from which one of the societies would emerge as dominant for a time.

At the beginning of the eighteenth century, another level of competition among societies was more basic. Some ways of life were themselves threatened. The Bushmen, a hunting-gathering people in Southwest Africa, in the words of a European observer, "are without chiefs, laws, Government or organization of any kind, so that no human power can save them from absorption, either by ourselves or by some powerful neighboring nation."[18] In the eighteenth century, peoples in scattered and relatively isolated regions still lived within this ancient framework for life. However, the hunter-gatherers faced farmers and herders whose

The Khoisan peoples of Southwest Africa were among the few remaining hunting-gathering peoples in the world of the eighteenth century. The numbers dwindled as farmers took over their hunting and gathering grounds. © The British Library Board

ways of life were created originally in the Agricultural Revolution, as early as 10,000 years ago. Over the centuries, the agriculturalists displaced or converted many of the hunting-gathering peoples in a great struggle which gradually was eliminating this way of life around the world.

The ways of life of the agriculturalists who still lived in small groups and were led by village or tribal chieftains were also under threat, as they had been for millennia. Although permanent small farming communities remained the home of the majority of humans, many of these communities were absorbed into or conquered by the city-based societies that began to develop almost five thousand years ago. The farmers were peasants living in the larger economic and political systems. The rulers viewed the peasants as ignorant and needing guidance, as reflected in a Chinese imperial edict of 1738: "The small farmers, in their ignorance, are eager only to sell [their harvest] in order to receive money on the spot, and do not think of laying in reserves for the remainder of the year."[19] In most societies, the farmers were viewed as drudges to be controlled by the political elites.

The pastoral nomadic peoples historically dominated the great plains and steppe areas of the world. Over the centuries, these peoples had interacted with the major urban agricultural societies. Sometimes this represented a cooperative relationship since the pastoral peoples often controlled the open regions through which trade passed. At the beginning of the eighteenth century, for example, Arab nomadic groups were important in maintaining the security of the Muslim pilgrimage routes between Damascus and the Holy Cities in Arabia. In other times, there was conflict and, from time to time, nomadic peoples successfully invaded and conquered urban-agricultural societies. The great historical steppe confederations of pastoral nomadic peoples in Central Asia were a threat to the major urban societies. Some of the major military campaigns of the Qing emperors in the first half of the eighteenth century were against the Zunghar confederation, possibly the last of these significant powers.

By 1700 this long competition among different ways of life reached a significant new stage. The hunting and gathering peoples were increasingly marginalized and remained significant only in isolated regions. As globalization intensified, the protection that isolation provided was being broken down. The primary areas remaining for the hunting and gathering peoples were the great rain forests of South America and Central Africa, especially in the Amazon and Congo river basins, the dry areas of southwestern Africa, especially in the Kalahari Desert, and the Arctic regions of North America and Eurasia. In these areas, farming and herding peoples encroached on lands necessary for hunting, and increasingly urban peoples came to the lands for exploitation of natural resources.

Some of the hunting peoples were themselves adopting agricultural methods that were changing them into pastoral and farming communities. The San peoples of the Kalahari region are a good example. They faced steady encroachment on their lands by migrating Bantu pastoral and farming peoples and, in the seventeenth century, by growing numbers of European, especially Dutch, farmers and traders.

The small agricultural communities also faced growing challenges from the expansion of urban societies but were in stronger positions than the gathering-hunting societies, especially in the global competitions with the urban civilizations. At the beginning of the eighteenth century, groups like the Wampanoag (a Native American people) in North America had been almost completely displaced from their farmlands by British colonists, including the Pilgrims of Massachusetts, while other groups farther west were organizing powerful confederations of tribes that, at least for a time, could slow the expansion of urban agricultural society. Nomadic pastoral-herding peoples and village agricultural communities from the steppes of Central Asia to the Great Plains of North America and the islands of the Pacific were increasingly drawn into the control of the large urban agricultural societies and were becoming parts of the large-scale networks of global trade.

The eighteenth century was a turning point for many of these peoples as the urban-agricultural civilizations expanded. At the beginning of the century, however, the domains of many of the nomadic and farming peoples still appeared to be secure, even though the dramatic changes were already underway. The chieftains of the Pacific prospered and were still isolated from much of the rest of the world. In the broad Pacific Ocean basin, the great sea peoples of Polynesia continued long voyages of exploration, settlement, and conquest. In island groups such as the Hawaiian Islands, ambitious chieftains battled for control, first of individual islands and then multi-island realms. In sub-Saharan Africa, strong ethnically based political systems and large trade networks continued to develop and prosper. The long-term damage that would be caused by the slave trade was not yet obvious. In possibly the most visible display of the continuing power of pastoral and agricultural peoples, the armed forces of a Central Asian people, the Manchus, conquered China. They brought an end to the Ming dynasty in 1644, and established their own dynasty, the Qing, which lasted until 1912.

The expansions of urban-agricultural societies by 1700, however, reflected their growing power compared with pastoral and agricultural peoples. With the strength provided by global economic expansions and gunpowder weaponry, the balance in the competition between urban societies and smaller agricultural societies was shifting decisively. The expansion of Chinese imperial power and urban society into Central Asia under the dynamic leadership of the Qing rulers, along with Russian expansion in the region, showed the new power of urban agricultural societies to control any threat from pastoralist confederations.

Russian imperial expansion into Central Asia from the west had already brought an end to a number of the states whose origins lay in the conquests of Mongol and Turkic peoples. In a rapid expansion across the northern stretches of Siberia, Russian pioneers reached the Pacific coast in 1637. This activity brought nomadic northern peoples under Russian control. The formal recognition of control of the vast Siberian regions by imperial forces came in 1689 with the Treaty of Nerchinsk, in which the Chinese and Russian Empires set their boundaries in the region.

The clash of urban and pastoral ways of life is visible in the description of the Central Asian nomadic life by an urban Jesuit who was part of a Chinese imperial delegation negotiating the Treaty of Nerchinsk with the Russians. Father Gerbillon wrote, "They lead a most slothful, lazy life, for they do nothing from one year's end to the other but feed their flocks of which they take little care, leaving them day and night grazing on the plains."[20] In this view, these people, like the Chinese peasants described in the Imperial Edict of 1738, needed strong guidance from a responsible urban authority.

The European settlers in North America still viewed the Native American peoples as strong rivals and possible partners. The Quaker community of Mary Morgan Pennell worked to establish constructive relations with its neighbors, the Delaware, and the Native Americans may have had a role to play in her vision of the "trying days" to come. Major Native American groups posed threats under specific local circumstances. However, the defeat of a major coalition of Native American peoples from most of New England in King Philip's War (1675–76) indicated the relative strengths and weaknesses of the new settler communities and the existing societies.

Leaders and thinkers in all of the large societies were engaged in redefining the nature of urban agricultural civilizations. In 1700, these efforts were often most visible in the careers of powerful rulers like Louis XIV in France, Peter the Great in Russia, the Kangxi emperor of China, and Awrangzib, the Mughal Sultan in India. However, the successes, and failures, of these prominent leaders were part of broader changes that were taking place in their societies and the broader world of which they were a part. The different ways in which their societies developed represent alternative ways of coping with the changing conditions of the time. The world at the beginning of the eighteenth century was a world in which four major urban civilizations—China, India, the Middle East, and Western Europe—were highly visible. Their internal developments and interactions with each other are an important theme of eighteenth-century history.

Imperial China in 1700 may have been the most powerful of the major urban societies of the time. In addition to the political changes instituted by the new Manchu rulers, China was experiencing significant social and economic changes. China was in the midst of a significant growth in population after a decline in the previous century. The emperor Kangxi noted in his tours of the countryside, "Obviously the population was increasing; but at the same time, the amount of land was not increasing."[21] Many Chinese moved outside of the traditional centers of population into regions in the central and western parts of the country, expanding the country's base of productivity and wealth. At least some of the increase in population was made possible by the introduction into Chinese agriculture of important new crops from the Western Hemisphere. Peanuts, maize (corn), sweet potatoes, and Andean potatoes could frequently be grown in land that had previously been marginally productive and provided a major increase in food available for rural peoples. For example, the ability of the Andean potato to be grown on hillsides assisted in the expanded settlement in the highland areas of the Yangzi River valley, which previously had relatively limited population.

At the center, the Qing dynasty provided leadership that brought peace and prosperity. In his valedictory edict issued in 1717, the Kangxi emperor could realistically and justifiably proclaim, "The country is more or less at peace and the world is at peace. Even if we haven't improved all manners and customs, and made all the people prosperous and contented, yet I have worked with unceasing diligence and intense watchfulness."[22] He consolidated central rule and presided over a major expansion of the empire. Extending beyond the borders of formal military and administrative control, the emperor was at the center of networks of tribute and trade extending from Central Asia and Korea to Vietnam and Java.

The definition of the new imperial system involved profound continuities with past Chinese institutions. The Chinese imperial cultural tradition had foundations in the classical empire of the Han dynasty (206 BCE–220 CE), which defined the Chinese ideal of empire. Qing leaders recognized longstanding Han Chinese traditions and ideals of political order and social harmony associated with the tradition of the moral philosopher Confucius (551–479 BCE). However, distinctive Manchu identities of language and culture were still, in 1700, strong among the ruling elite. The Kangxi emperor noted differences between Manchus and Chinese in this elite: "The Manchus are direct and open, whereas the Chinese think it better not to let any joy or anger show in their faces. And the Manchus are often tougher and braver than the Chinese Bannermen."[23] This recognition of diversity within the ruling group reflects an important characteristic of the developing Chinese model of civilizational organization. The emperor was not saying that the differences are bad, only that they exist. The Chinese model includes many elements of social and cultural diversity which are accepted or tolerated as long as the primacy of the major Han and Confucian traditions was recognized. In this framework, it was possible for the Kangxi emperor to include Jesuit scholars in his court and to encourage their scientific work, as long as they recognized Confucian traditions.

One important aspect of continuity is that in China the empire's borders largely coincided with the geographical region in which Chinese language and culture predominated. In the era of the classical empires of Rome, Persia, Han China, and Mauryan and Gupta India, the cultural identity of these empires was associated the cultural traditions of major regions that they ruled. However, in 1700 China was relatively distinctive in this regard. The Chinese mode of civilization at the beginning of the eighteenth century involved a sense of identity between areas under Chinese political control and areas where Chinese language and culture were major elements in local culture. The Chinese style created a prosperous and powerful society that was at least the equal of the other major urban-agricultural societies of the time in terms of economic strength and socio-political development.

Descendants of warriors from Central Asia also ruled most of India in 1700, but their dynasty, the Mughals, was past its days of greatest power. The Mughals established Muslim rule in India in the sixteenth century, but rulers like Sultan Akbar (r.1556–1605) developed an administrative system and an elite culture that included important non-Muslim Indian traditions. At the beginning of the eighteenth century, the Mughal ruler was Awrangzib (r.1658–1707), who came to the throne by rebelling against his father, Shah Jahan, in 1658. His long rule was characterized by almost constant warfare. He imposed a more exclusively Islamic vision of society, departing from the more pluralist traditions of Akbar's rule. While this strengthened his support among the Muslim scholars, it aroused the militant opposition of important non-Muslim groups. By 1700, the Mughal state was still a major power, but much of its resources had been spent in fighting wars.

South Asian society prospered in many ways, however. The Indian economy flourished under Mughal rule and the production of textiles made Indian merchants and entrepreneurs (such as Mulla Abdul Ghafur) major actors in vast networks of world trade. Trade in the Indian Ocean basin was an important part of the global networks. No single power dominated the region militarily, and Europeans did not control the regional trade. In 1700 the great Dutch and British trading companies were still only limited parts of the broader patterns of commerce. British trading houses in major Indian ports such as Surat and Bombay worked with Indian merchants and producers. Individual adventurers, among them a Scot, Alexander Hamilton, joined regional merchants in what was called the "country trade," as well as from time to time working for

Awrangzib Alamgir led the Mughal Empire in India through an era of expansion and civil wars. His policies emphasized the empire's Muslim identity, leading to disunity as the empire began to face the growing power of the European trade companies in South Asia. © The Trustees of the British Museum. All rights reserved the British East India Company.[24] Even though the Mughal state was weaker than it had been, no foreign group was in a position yet to dominate the sultans. Instead, at times the British East India Company came to provide important support for Mughal administration.

The emerging style of Indian civilization was very different from that of China. One imperial court did not rule all of India; the Mughals always faced smaller regional powers, some of whom were not Muslim. Although the Mughals, like the Qing, were in origin culturally different from the majority of their subjects, unlike the Qing, the Mughals did not adopt the basic political culture of the majority that they ruled. Though some Mughal rulers included Hindus in leadership positions in the empire, they did not include Hindu political concepts in the political ideals of the sultanate. However, the rule of the sultans recognized significant local and regional autonomies. This opened the way for a broad range of economic activities and considerable religious diversity. Relations with Europeans and others were often competitive but still constructive. The style seemed well suited to the interactions in the Indian Ocean world of 1700.

Indian civilization is built on foundations going back to ancient times. Distinctive Hindu traditions with great religious and literary classics go back to the second millennium BCE, and India is the region where Buddhism developed. However, by 1700, it was also an important part of the broader world of Islam. The Islamic world included the core region of Middle Eastern civilization and extended from Southeast and Central Asia to West Africa. In this broader hemispheric world, distinctive local and regional expressions of Islam blended with a more trans-regional and cosmopolitan sense of belonging to a greater human community of faith. Already by 1700, Muslims in India were influential in the development of Muslim mystic brotherhoods and in shaping intellectual studies of the traditions of the Prophet Muhammad and in Qur'anic interpretation.

One of the major Muslim empires at the end of the seventeenth century, the Safavid dynasty in Iran, was losing control of its territory. The Safavids had restored political unity to historic Persia by conquests in the sixteenth century. They established Shi'ism, an important Islamic sectarian tradition, as the religion of the state. By 1700, the dynasty was plagued by internal divisions and attacks from Central Asia. Civil wars and invasions, in the words of a Polish Jesuit observer, reduced what he called "one of the most flourishing Monarchies in Asia" to "a desolate Wilderness."[25] Safavid dynastic rule came to an end when Nadir, a Turkoman military commander, took control of the state and proclaimed himself to be Shah of Iran in 1736.

The Ottoman Empire, the second major Middle Eastern state in 1700, was a great power. Its ruling elite had roots in Turkish warriors and nomads who came to the Middle East in medieval times. They established a state in the Muslim tradition of rule by sultans, military rulers supported by religious authority. The Ottoman Turkish conquest of Constantinople in 1453 made the empire the heir to Eastern Roman or Byzantine imperial traditions as well as the most prominent Muslim state. By 1700 it controlled most of the Arabic-speaking world and Anatolia and was a major European power. Ottoman forces laid siege to Vienna in 1683 and the empire ruled most of the Balkan Peninsula. Although the Ottomans were no longer as clearly dominant in the Mediterranean region as they had been in the sixteenth century, they were among the great powers of the day.

The Ottoman ruling elite was a distinctive group somewhat set apart from the broader society by special court language and customs. The core of the state was the sultan, his palace establishment in Istanbul, and his governors and garrisons in the provinces. Although the institutions of government—judicial, educational, administrative—were large, the subject populations had a relatively high degree of autonomy in local affairs. This was specially true for the non-Muslim peoples, with such institutions as the Greek Orthodox Church maintaining effective control over their communities.

Ottoman military losses in the late seventeenth century provided impetus for active reform efforts. The grand vizier in 1700, Husayn Pasha of the prominent Köprülü family, reorganized the navy, replacing oar-powered galleys with sail-powered ships, significantly reduced sinecures in the army, and worked to reduce corruption and increase efficiency in the administrative scribal service. The results were reflected in the Ottoman victory over the army of Peter the Great in 1711, the occasion for a later grand vizier's cup of coffee with the king of Sweden.

The early eighteenth century also witnessed a continuation of participation in world trade by Middle Eastern merchants. The city of Izmir (Smyrna) was emerging as a major economic center, and older cities like Aleppo, Cairo, and Istanbul continued to be prosperous. Smyrna, for example, was a distribution center for local textiles like angora wool and products from the mohair-producing center in Ankara, and it became, in the eighteenth century, a major transit center in the silk trade. Cairo was a significant center in the coffee trade. The Ottoman provinces, in both the Arab world and the Balkans, were prospering from the increasing volume of interregional trade.

The Muslim world extended beyond the Middle East and South Asia into sub-Saharan Africa and Central and Southeast Asia. The general pattern of a ruler (usually titled a sultan) managing a small military and administrative elite as they ruled a diverse urban-agricultural society provided a successful way of controlling many different regions. In West Africa, the last of the large medieval empires, the Songhay, was replaced by clusters of city-states that were turbulent but prosperous, engaging in active interregional trade. The Portuguese presence in East Africa came to an end with the capture of Fort Jesus in Mombasa in 1698 by the rising power in the western Indian Ocean of the sultans of Oman. In Southeast Asia, the activities of itinerant Muslim scholars and teachers consolidated the position of Islam in the region and an expansion of commercial activity provided the economic base for a series of powerful sultanates in Malacca, Banten, and Aceh. By 1700 the growing power of European trading companies in the region, especially the Dutch East India Company, meant a decline in the power of the local sultans but not an end to the cultural expansion of Islam.

The experience of Muslims as they participated in the annual ritual of pilgrimage (hajj) to Mecca reflects the special character of the global Muslim community. Since Muslims are required, if possible, to undertake the Hajj at least once during their lifetime, Muslims come to Mecca from all over the world. Traveling scholars like the Moroccan Abdullah al-'Ayyashi in the late seventeenth century could note differences in religious customs and claim that "Common people, Arabs and Berbers, in our Morocco, are *faqihs* [*certified legal scholars*] in comparison with them [the tribal peoples of western and central Arabia],"[26] but he still felt that he was within the greater Muslim community. This balance between local diversities and a broader sense of shared religious identity was characteristic of the Muslim world at the beginning of the eighteenth century.

The emerging Western pattern was similar. In Western Europe, there was no single unifying imperial system equivalent to the Confucian order in China. The Protestant Reformation of the sixteenth century and the destructive religious wars of the seventeenth century weakened the foundations for such a unity. In 1700, the efforts of Louis XIV of France to dominate, if not rule, Europe were beginning to unravel. The political order of Western Europe was one of warring states that occasionally, through grand alliances and congresses, could establish some order and stability. The negotiations in 1648 at the end of the disastrous Thirty Years War produced the Treaties of Westphalia, which were considered throughout the eighteenth century, in the words of an observer in 1800, "as the bulwarks of the public law of Europe,"[27] setting many of the foundations for the Western system of international relations in the modern era.

In the Western Hemisphere, European settler colonies were well established by the beginning of the eighteenth century. The largest of the newly established societies were in Central and South America under Spanish and Portuguese control, with distinctive social orders. In 1700, indigenous peoples, even in the areas that had been the great urban agricultural empires of the Aztecs and Incas, became primarily a lower class of laborers and peasants. They were not, however, displaced or eliminated as they ultimately were in North America. The territories were ruled by an immigrant elite that, by 1700, was divided between a developing local (creole/*criollo*) upper class of descendants of earlier immigrants and the continuing stream of new officials coming from the Iberian Peninsula (*peninsulares*). Other major groups in the complicated class structure were people of mixed racial ancestry and Africans, who primarily formed an enslaved laboring class.

By the eighteenth century the Creole-Peninsulares rivalry became a major feature in colonial society. Already in the seventeenth century, a sense of a distinctive Creole identity emerged. In an early statement of this developing elite identity, a Creole Franciscan priest wrote a history of the "New World" in which he claimed that children born in the New World "are born with such noble spirits that since they are born here, no one is inclined to learn the mechanical trades and arts that their fathers brought from Spain . . . because this Peruvian sky and climate ennobles their aspirations and thoughts."[28] This aristocratic tone of this affirmation of identity emphasizes that the Creole upper class was no longer a working class and that newcomers from the homeland were expected to learn the "mechanical trades." Creole activism became, by the end of the eighteenth century, an important factor in the rise of "nationalist" revolutions in Latin America.

In most of the world, by 1700 the era of Spanish and Portuguese pre-eminence had passed and the Dutch, British, and French were only beginning to emerge as global economic powers. In Europe itself, the centers of economic power shifted from Mediterranean and Iberian states to northern Europe, as illustrated by the rise of Amsterdam and London as centers of finance and commerce and the parallel decline of the older Mediterranean trading centers such as Genoa. In the other regions of the Eastern Hemisphere, Western Europeans were increasingly active, but, like the Jesuits in the court of the Kangxi emperor, they were still minor actors in the broader socio-economic and political developments of the time. All of these developments created a dynamically changing collection of peoples and states in Western Europe, but it was not clear in 1700 that the somewhat chaotic Western mode of organizing society and state would lead the West into an era of global dominance.

This era was not a time of highly visible "clash of civilizations." Most of the major conflicts leading up to 1700 were internal: the Thirty Years War and the wars aroused by French expansionism under Louis XIV, the revolts and wars fought by Awrangzib in India, and Manchu pacification. The major conflicts across civilizations' boundaries were those between the Ottoman Empire and European states. However, these wars show that civilizational differences were not as significant as they might appear to later observers.

Human societies in 1700 around the globe were changing in many different ways. Hunting and gathering peoples and small agricultural communities show the continuing connections with peoples of antiquity. However, the changes in their relations with large urban societies provide a strong indication of important global changes. Among the major urban societies, continuities and transformations shape emerging alternative ways of organizing political authority and economic life in large urban societies. The discussions among Chinese scholars and Jesuits in the court of the Kangxi emperor involved new scientific concepts while the Qing dynasty was restoring longstanding Chinese imperial power. The prosperity and productivity of the Indian textile industry, as seen in the wealth of merchants like Mulla Abdul Ghafur of Surat, shows the growing strength of the networks of interregional trade. The religious message of a frontier preacher like Mary Morgan Pennell in Pennsylvania reflects the dual nature of developments. The Quaker movement of which she was a part arose in the distinctive seventeenth-century context of the English Civil War but the message of the coming of the end of history has deep roots in popular religious feelings and was part of the expectations of many peoples around the world.

Major institutions in the large urban societies were not yet modern but they were also no longer medieval. Ways of organizing large-scale societies competed for dominance. The stage was set for a century of expected change and unexpected transformations. At the beginning of the century, the major urban agricultural societies were roughly equal in power and wealth. Few futurists in 1700 could have predicted the major changes that would take place in the following century. An apocalyptic transformation did occur, but it took forms that were inconceivable to the secular and religious prophets of that day.

CHAPTER 2

Climaxes and New Beginnings

The "whole World as to Trade, is but as one Nation or People, and therein Nations are as Persons,"[1] wrote Roger North (1653–1734), a lawyer from a politically prominent British family, as he viewed the world at the end of the seventeenth century. This vision reflected the increasing globalization of economic enterprise at the beginning of the eighteenth century. Important merchants and commercial entrepreneurs during the eighteenth century managed worldwide economic networks. The North family itself invested in Russia, the Ottoman Empire, Africa, and the East Indies. Significant economic exchange among the world regions was not new, but it intensified throughout the eighteenth century.

Earlier inter-regional trade was largely in the hands of entrepreneurial adventurers like the North family. However, by the beginning of the eighteenth century, many of the formerly exotic products were staples of daily life and their production was central to economic and social structures in societies around the world. The individualistic adventurers were being replaced by large trading companies, in which later generations of the North family and others like them invested.

Large-scale production of certain key products like sugar, coffee, tobacco, and cotton created new wealth. John Oldmixon, an English historian at that time, describes the life of the new economic elite created by this wealth in Jamaica in 1708, noting the "Masters of Families in *Jamaica*, Planters and Merchants, live with as much Pomp and Pleasure, as any Gentlemen in the World; they keep their Coaches and six horses, have their Train of Servants in Liveries, running before and behind them."[2] The rise to this level of wealth was rapid, since these families had been involved in Jamaican economic life for less than half a century. However, the market for sugar, a major product of Jamaica, expanded rapidly. By the beginning of the eighteenth century, Oldmixon wrote, "Of all our *American* Commerce that of Sugar is most valuable, because most necessary."[3]

The production of sufficient quantities of products like sugar, tobacco, coffee, and cotton to meet the growing demand depended upon the establishment of large plantations. These plantations were a form of agricultural mass production that relied upon the availability of large numbers of field laborers. In the Caribbean and elsewhere, plantations came to depend upon enslaved workers, creating societies like Jamaica, which had "three sorts of Inhabitants, Masters, Servants and Slaves."[4] The products of the plantations were goods that needed to be exported and sold for cash. As a result, plantation owners were also deeply involved in international marketing and finance, making the plantations an important part of the emerging global economy.

Along with important changes in global economic life, reform movements and global interrelations were changing political and religious life as well. The great empires strengthened their central administrative structures and movements of religious renewal and reform reshaped religious life in many areas. Experiences in the Ottoman Empire and kingdom of Kongo illustrate the consequences of the longer-term developments in politics and religion.

Sultan Ahmad III came to the throne of the Ottoman Empire in 1703 as a result of a major rebellion and was deposed in another rebellion in 1730. He was heir to the line of sultans stretching back to the founding generations of the empire in the fourteenth century. The Ottoman state began as a small warrior state in western Anatolia and became a major world empire, symbolized by the conquest of Constantinople (Istanbul or Islambul in Ottoman usage since the conquest) in 1453. During the sixteenth century Ottomans conquered much of southeastern Europe and the Arab world, and by the seventeenth century, Ottoman rulers faced the challenges of maintaining this vast empire and consolidating administration, rather than expansion. The rebellions that brought Ahmad III to the throne and then deposed him were a part of this process of reshaping the Ottoman imperial system, with the bureaucratic and military leaders replacing the sultans as the center of power and policy.

Viewed in its own terms, the time of Ahmad III's rule is an era of dynamic activity in the reshaping of state and society. Ahmad III's predecessor, his brother Mustafa II, lost a war to a coalition of European states. The Treaty of Karlowitz (1699) at the end of that war was a major turning point in the Ottoman role in world affairs, as Ottoman weakness was now obvious to all. However, less than a decade after coming to power, the armies of Sultan Ahmad III won a major victory over the Russians at Prut in 1711 and much land that had been ceded to Russia at Karlowitz was restored.

If the empire was in significant decline, it was not obvious to many informed observers. Lady Mary Wortley Montagu, the wife of the British ambassador to the court of Ahmad III noted that "Military Discipline, such as now practis'd in Christendom, does not mightily suit them [the Ottomans]," but attributed this to the circumstance that "A long Peace has plung'd them into universal Sloth. . . . But, to make Amends, the Sciences flourish among them."[5]

The second half of Ahmad III's reign, known as the Tulip Period, was a time of great cultural and economic productivity. Textile and porcelain production expanded, and poets and scientists received patronage from the palace. In 1727 the first Muslim printing press in Turkey was established, initially publishing a major dictionary and books on history, geography, and some sciences. The era's symbol was the "tulipmania" that became the fashion among the wealthy, who imported expensive bulbs from the Netherlands. This trade is an interesting confirmation of the interconnections of the world of trade, since it mirrors a similar tulip-mania in the Netherlands in the early seventeenth century, when Europeans began to import tulips from Turkey.

Ahmad III and the empire that he ruled at the beginning of the eighteenth century was a major world power among the empires of the time. It built an increasingly centralized state but was not developing as a modern-style nation-state. The Ottomans recognized distinctive rights for minorities but were not laying foundations for a modern-style democracy. It was a time of consolidation, not expansion, and of reform rather than dramatic innovation. It was a distinctive time, neither medieval nor modern.

A religious movement in Kongo in west central Africa reflects major religious reforming trends of the time. At the beginning of the eighteenth century, Kongo was a monarchy ruled by a Catholic king with close ties to the Portuguese monarchy and the Catholic Church, whose subjects included many African Christians. In 1704, a young Christian woman saw a vision of a man dressed in the habit of a Capuchin monk. He proclaimed to this woman, Dona Beatriz Kimpa Vita, that he was Saint Antony, saying, "I have been sent from God to your head to preach to the people."[6] Dona Beatriz preached his message of unity and peace in a time of civil war in Kongo leading a movement of religious revival that attracted thousands of people. However, her teachings were viewed by church leaders as heretical and in 1706 she was burned at the stake.

St. Anthony, represented in this brass pendant from Kongo, was seen in visions by Dona Beatriz Kimpa Vita in the early eighteenth century. The movement that she led combined Christian and African religious themes and was a major political force in the kingdom of Kongo until she was executed for heresy in 1706. © The Metropolitan Museum of Art / Art Resource, NY

Although her ministry was short, her movement shaped political and religious institutions in the region. Christianity was more than two centuries old in Kongo and a great king, Afonso Mbemba Nzinga, had become Christian at the beginning of the sixteenth century. The monarchy was closely tied to Portuguese commercial interests and the Catholic Church. By the end of the seventeenth century, the slave trade and civil war brought chaos to the country. The Antonian movement of Dona Beatriz sought to bring an end to both civil conflict and the slave trade but along the way, it came into conflict with both the monarchy and the church.

In the context of the broad global interactions of the time, she combined Christian and local elements in a new cosmopolitan synthesis in which she could proclaim: "There are black Kongolese up in heaven. . . . But . . . they are not black in color nor white, because in Heaven no one has any color."[7] European church leaders might condemn this type of activity, which they considered to be heretical syncretism. A leading church official in Kongo, for example, declared that Dona Beatriz's major prayer, the Salva Antoniana, contained "so many outrageous statements that I do not know if I should call them diabolical craziness or truly desecrating blasphemy."[8] However, by the eighteenth century, despite traditional institutional limitations, global interactions were creating significant local syntheses around the world, producing new religious organizations as well as new economic and political organizations. Her movement was one among many at the beginning of the eighteenth century that challenged and redefined major traditions and structures of faith.

The North family, Sultan Ahmad III, and Dona Beatriz are part of dynamic global developments in economics, politics, and religion. These changes often involved adventurers and novelty in the early days. Military opportunists and economic speculators laid the foundations for the one world of trade in which entrepreneurs like the North family could work with people like Mulla Abdul Ghafur, a major Indian cotton merchant. Increasingly effective use of gunpowder weaponry and more efficiently centralized administration supporting standing armies changed the modes of warfare.

The long competition between urban-agricultural societies and both hunting-gathering societies and the small agricultural communities of farming villagers and pastoral herding peoples entered a significant new stage. The domination of cities and urban societies over the other types of societies was becoming clear in the first decades of the eighteenth century. Hunting-gathering peoples had long been under pressure from other groups and were significant only in isolated and environmentally marginal places by the eighteenth century. The principal areas were the Arctic regions of North America and Eurasia, the dry areas of southern Africa, especially in the Kalahari Desert, Australia, and the great rain forest regions of Africa and South America. In each of these areas, expansion of major urban powers significantly reduced the amount of territory for gathering and hunting.

Some of the most important transformations of hunting-gathering peoples were in the Arctic regions. As major states developed more coordinated power and as economic entrepreneurs organized in increasingly efficient large companies, Arctic peoples came under growing pressures. The Sami people in far northern Europe lived for many centuries as fishermen and hunters closely tied to reindeer herds. As Scandinavian states became more effectively organized and Sweden became a major

military power by the seventeenth century, the Sami peoples came under pressure to pay taxes in monetary currency and much of their land was confiscated by the expanding states. Although the changes had begun, it was still possible, early in the eighteenth century, for a Swedish scientific observer, Carl von Linné (Linnaeus), to describe their life in hunting-gathering terms: "Their soil is unwounded by the plough. . . . They wander from place to place, live in tents, lead the patriarchal life of shepherds of old."[9] However, by the end of the century, most of the surviving Samis were small-scale agriculturalists engaged in reindeer husbandry or peasant-style farming.

All across the Arctic regions, similar changes occurred. In the sixteenth century, the newly reorganized Russian state began significant eastward expansion, with Russian frontier people and merchants reaching the Pacific by 1637. The expanding Russian and Chinese Empires established an imperial division of central and northern Asia by agreement at Nerchinsk in 1689. This left the new Russian Empire in control of the territories of virtually all of the Asian Arctic gathering-hunting peoples. While ethnic identities were sometimes preserved, the groups were incorporated into the Russian systems of economic life and political-military control—and they ceased to be hunting-gathering peoples. In North America, the development of the fur trade brought indigenous people in the northern regions into the growing global trade networks. Begun by individual adventurers, by the early eighteenth century the fur trade was increasingly controlled by large companies like the British Hudson's Bay Company. The societies of hunters and small-scale agriculturalists were significantly changed by the products that they received in this trade, notably guns and iron tools.

Elsewhere hunting-gathering peoples faced similar pressures. In 1500, southern Africa had little contact with other world regions; but by 1700, the region was an active part of global networks of trade and power. Migrations of African agriculturalists into the region forced many local hunting-gathering peoples either to adapt to agricultural life or move to environmentally marginal areas. Dutch colonists from the settlement at the Cape of Good Hope, established in the seventeenth century, also expanded the areas in which they farmed. Some of the San and other local peoples continued to maintain a hunting-gathering way of life in some isolated areas, but in smaller numbers than ever before. A Swedish traveler in the eighteenth century described the situation of these so-called Bushmen dramatically: These people "are sworn enemies to the pastoral life . . . and are pursued and exterminated like wild beasts, whose manners they have assumed."[10] In the forests and savannas of central Africa the expansions of trade networks and local chieftain-cies incorporated growing numbers of hunting-gathering peoples. Pygmy hunters were, for example, important suppliers of ivory in international trade networks.

Well-organized chieftaincies flourished in smaller non-urban agricultural societies in the early years of the eighteenth century. Often they were expanding at the expense of hunting-gathering peoples and less well-organized farming groups. These chieftaincies were sometimes in frontier regions of expanding urban societies, as in central Asia and North America, while others developed in relatively isolated areas.

Maritime networks and major chieftaincies in the central Pacific basin remained relatively untouched by global developments at the beginning of the eighteenth century. They were not yet a part of the trans-Pacific networks involving trade between Spanish colonies in the Western Hemisphere and the Philippines and East Asia. Many were not "discovered" by Europeans until later in the eighteenth century. However, in island groups like the Hawaiian archipelago, chieftaincies consolidated their control over major islands and, at the beginning of the eighteenth century, were expanding their networks of control to neighboring islands.

In many areas of Africa, smaller agricultural chieftaincies consolidated control over larger areas and important regional monarchies like the Kingdom of Kongo developed in western, central, and eastern Africa. Often interregional and global trade relations acted as a catalyst in this process. The growing Atlantic slave trade, for example, is an important part of this consolidation of chieftaincy power in some areas, providing local rulers with the weapons and wealth necessary to conquer and control their neighbors. In the commercial cities of East Africa, trade in cotton cloth from India (involving merchants like Abdul Ghafur of Surat) was an important element in the economy of the Swahili coast. By the beginning of the eighteenth century, large monarchies and wealthy city-states were a significant part of African life, transforming and displacing many of the older small agricultural and herding societies.

Major northern American peoples experienced similar development of larger social and political units. As European colonists moved inland from their coastal settlements they interacted with a variety of native groups. Some of the Native American societies remained basically small agricultural communities. However, in some areas large confederations of peoples represented new ways of organizing political and economic life. The Iroquois Confederation emerged as a significant power in the Great Lakes region by the beginning of the eighteenth century. In treaty negotiations with Europeans in 1744, a major chief described the establishment of this confederation: "Our wise forefathers established union and amity between the Five Nations; this has made us formidable; this has given us great weight and authority with our neighboring nations."[11] Benjamin Franklin was among the European negotiators and he agreed that this league was an effective form of union.[12] The unification of the Mohawk, Oneida, Onondaga, Cayuga, and Seneca nations (along with the Tuscarora after 1722) created a powerful alliance that dominated the region.

The Iroquois were active partners in the trans-Atlantic fur trade, which provided them with added economic strength and firearms. In the early eighteenth century, the vast region west of the Appalachian Mountains was the scene of a series of conflicts for control among the Iroquois, French, and British. The continuing power of the Iroquois in these wars shows that at least in some areas the large chieftaincies could still compete with the forces of urban agricultural societies.

The most visible success of smaller agricultural-nomadic societies at the beginning of the eighteenth century is in China. Chinese imperial dynasties faced pressure from the great chieftaincies of central Asia for thousands of years. Mongols in the era of Genghis Khan and his grandson Kublai Khan in the thirteenth century CE conquered China and established the Yuan dynasty (1260–1368 CE). The last of the great central Asian conquests of China is in the seventeenth century, when the Manchus gained control over all of the lands of the old empire and established the last of the imperial dynasties, the Qing (1644–1911).

The Manchus were not simple nomadic invaders. They were heirs to a long tradition of interactions with the Chinese Empire and, before the conquests, ruled a complex major chieftaincy on the empire's northern and western borders. As Qing emperors, they maintained the Chinese bureaucratic system of civil administration managed by officials selected on the basis of traditional examinations, but they added Manchu supervisors for imperial policy implementation. The Qing also established a military system that maintained both Chinese and Manchu units under Manchu command. Through policies like these, the Qing quickly established a synthesis of Chinese and Manchu ruling cultures and practice that gave added strength to the Chinese imperial system itself, but it also marked the end of the threat of invasion by nomadic chieftaincies and confederations.

The careers of a number of highly visible rulers of large states in major urban societies illustrate some of the major themes of politics at the beginning of the eighteenth century. Sultan Ahmad III (r. 1703–30) is only one of a number of major rulers whose reigns at the beginning of the century set the tone for politics. During his period of rule there was a continuing struggle to redefine the nature of the Ottoman Empire, which at this time controlled much of southeastern Europe as well as most of the Arab world. Eighteenth-century observers tended to view the coups that brought Ahmad to power in 1703 and overthrew him in 1730 as dynastic disputes similar to such conflicts in other European monarchies rather than reflecting changes in the political system. For example, Voltaire, in his book *Candide*, presents a fictional account of a gathering of six deposed monarchs in the early eighteenth century in an inn. He has Ahmed III say, "I was Grand Sultan for many years; I dethroned my brother, my nephew dethroned me, my viziers lost their heads, and I am condemned to end my days in the old seraglio [palace]."[13] However, these dynastic conflicts were part of the reshaping of political society in which local and regional groups had significant autonomy within the framework of a central administrative system.

A remarkable set of rulers of the time—the Kangxi emperor in China, Awrangzib in South Asia, Peter the Great in Russia, and Louis XIV in France—shows the changing nature of great states and empires in the different major regions. These states were basically dynastic and imperial, and most ruling elites had little cultural or social identification with their subjects. The European ruling elite was cosmopolitan, described by the nineteenth-century British historian William Makepeace Thackeray: "whilst common men were driven off by herds, and sold to fight. . ., noblemen passed from court to court, seeking service with one prince or the other."[14] Even where there was some sense of a broader cultural identification between ruler and ruled, the era of the integrated "nation-state" in which the political system is identified with the national culture of the people was still in the future.

In China, the Manchu conquest in the seventeenth century brought new military vitality to the old empire. The new rulers of the Qing dynasty maintained many of the older patterns of rule in the Confucian framework, which had taken many forms since the imperial unification of China almost two thousand years earlier. The second Manchu ruler, the Kangxi emperor (r. 1662–1722), completed the consolidation of Qing rule throughout China by 1700. He gave added strength to the examination system that was the heart of Chinese traditions of administrative efficiency. He established the Qing imperial system as an effective synthesis of Manchu and Confucian traditions and he actively encouraged Jesuits from Europe to participate in the intellectual life of his realm. By the time of his death in 1722, Chinese rule or direct influence stretched from the territories in Siberia and the northeast to Tibet and Taiwan, possibly the largest extent of Chinese imperial rule in history. The strength of this centralized Qing system placed China among the truly major powers of the early eighteenth century.

In South Asia, Awrangzib came to the throne of the Mughal Empire, the Muslim sultanate that had dominated India since the early sixteenth century. He took control of a wealthy empire including most of northern India in 1658. By his death in 1707 his empire had expanded to include the Deccan and much of southern India, but was weakened by the long series of wars of conquest and suppression of numerous revolts.

The Mughals were a Muslim minority ruling a large and diverse population with a Hindu majority. Awrangzib's predecessors, especially his great grandfather Akbar (r. 1556–1605), tended to adopt policies that gave recognition to this diversity, but Awrangzib's reputation is, in the laudatory words of his official court biography, that "he was characterized by perfect devotion to the rites of the Faith."[15] In practice, this meant that he imposed restrictions on non-Muslims, such as limiting or prohibiting the construction of new Hindu temples and destroying a number of important existing temples. As a part of his emphasis on the Muslim character of his regime, he supported and supervised the collection of a major compendium of legal opinions from scholars and judges of the Hanafi school of Islamic law, *al-Fatawa al-Alamgiriyya*. This collection provided a legal base for unity of Sunni Muslims in South Asia and became famous in other parts of the Muslim world. On the long run, this effort to strengthen the cohesion of the ruling group weakened the empire.

Russia was a new and rising empire at the beginning of the eighteenth century. Initially the rulers of Moscow fought long wars against remnants of the old Mongol Empire and surrounding states like Sweden and Poland. The Moscovite princes proclaimed themselves the rulers of all Russia but faced the competition of a powerful landed nobility and an influential church. In a time of civil wars in 1613, an assembly of the land-controlling notables and church officials elected Michael Romanov as monarch (czar). During the following century, the new Romanov dynasty consolidated the power of the monarchy but faced many challenges ranging from peasant revolts and internal religious divisions to wars with neighboring powers. The rule of Peter the Great (r. 1689–1725) began the transformation of this turbulent state from simply one among many monarchies ruling smaller societies in eastern Europe into the dominant power in the region and beyond.

Peter the Great's policies involved bringing the landed nobility and the church under the control of the central monarchy. His major vehicle for this effort was a program of extensive reforms building on the examples of emerging centralized monarchies in northern and western Europe. In 1697–98, at the age of twenty-five, he went on an extended trip to western Europe, where he examined political, military, and economic institutions. What he learned provided some of the foundations for a program of important changes in social and political institutions. This program and vision reduced the power of the old nobility by replacing many of the older assemblies and honorary positions with central administrative bureaus. He dramatically reorganized the church by bringing the old patriarchate into a central government ministry. Feofan Prokopovich, a major leader in the reorganized Orthodox Church, emphasized Peter the Great's dramatic leadership in his funeral eulogy: "O Russia, he is your Moses. . . . O Russia, he is your Solomon. . . . He is also, O Russian Church, your David and Constantine."[16] His programs had many opponents, but they also recognized that he had radically changed Russia.

In China, India, and the Middle East, society and politics were dominated by single major political systems. But in Europe by contrast, the basic structure of politics was dominated by a network of emerging and competing smaller dynastic states bound together by some shared religious traditions, economic relations, and an emerging system of interstate relations created by a series of treaties following major continental wars. From time to time, one state would attempt to impose an imperial unity on the European network of states, but such efforts failed. The long history of the Holy Roman Empire bore witness to that history and in the sixteenth century the Hapsburgs came close to establishing such a hegemony. However, that ambitious venture collapsed by the middle of the seventeenth century and new competitors emerged, often associated with more distinctive cultural, proto-"national" identities like the French monarchy.

The French king Louis XIV (r. 1643–1715) was the architect of the French dominance in Europe by the end of the seventeenth century. His long reign began in the midst of major European religious wars and the Fronde (1648–53), a major rebellion of nobles against the centralizing monarchy in France. The French style of monarchy became the model for the emerging European goal of strong centralized states. France expanded territorially through conquests in the Netherlands and the Rhinelands and was the central power in a network of alliances of

Peter the Great in Russia worked to strengthen the power of the monarchy by reducing the power of the nobility. Political cartoons like this one highlighted his measures to force a Westernization of appearance by taxing the traditional long beards of the old aristocrats. HIP/Art Resource, NY

major powers. France appeared on the brink of realizing the old vision of Europe dominated by a single center of power.

The French state was dynastic but it was based on a central administrative system, so that the individual monarch was not as important as the state structure. Louis XIV emphasized this priority in his dying

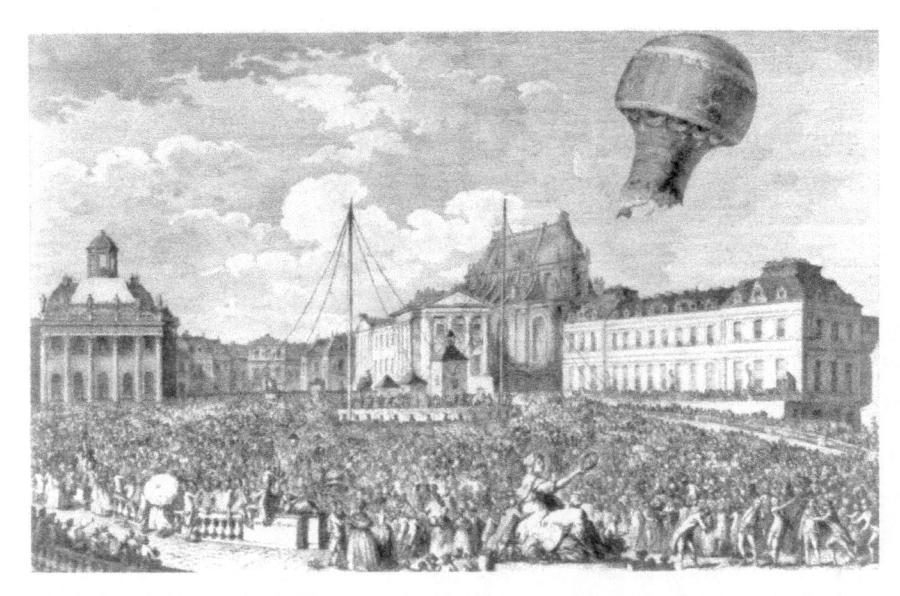

The palace in Versailles, built by Louis XIV, became a symbol of monarchical power. Events at the palace throughout the eighteenth century, like this experiment with a hot air balloon in 1783, show the patronage for the new sciences by the centralizing monarchies. Library of Congress Prints and Photographs Division

words, as reported by a witness, "I depart, but the State shall always remain."[17] Most scholars agree that he did not make the more personalized authoritarian identification of himself with the state, in the often-quoted statement, "L'État, c'est moi" ("The state, that is me").

This new style of state could not claim authority over all of "European civilization" and was, in this way, different from the Chinese imperial state and the other major regional empires. Instead, European civilization became a network of competing states that claimed sovereignty within the borders of the territories defined by their dynastic claims and military power. They interacted with other European states in a series of major wars and alliances to maintain a rough balance of power. The major war among the European states at the beginning of the eighteenth century, the War of the Spanish Succession (1701–14), brought an end to the expansion efforts of Louis XIV. The idea of a single power dominating all of Europe was replaced, in the words of explanatory letters associated with the Treaty of Utrecht (1713) by a recognition of the "Maxim of securing for ever the universal Good and Quiet of Europe, by an equal weight of power" among the major states.[18]

The emerging European-style state in this model had a strong, centralized administrative structure supporting a dynasty associated in some way with a distinctive cultural and linguistic identity. It was not a "nation-state," but the developing dynastic state had some growing identification with a "nation" associated with the subject populations. The idea of a "nation" as a separate human community having the right to determine its political destiny was beginning to be an important part of European political ideology. In some countries, parliaments began to take the role of speaking for the nation. However, even where some feelings of "national" identities were beginning to develop, ruling elites in the monarchies continued to be cosmopolitan and royal families were frequently related by marriage.

The blending together of dynastic and national politics can be seen in the emergence of the United Kingdom of Great Britain. In Britain, as a result of a major civil war in the seventeenth century and subsequent political developments, ultimate political authority passed from the monarch to the sovereign national parliament. The elected parliament maintained the monarchy but had control over the dynastic succession. The national parliament in 1701 determined the line of succession would be through the German House of Hanover (descendants of the seventeenth-century King James I) to ensure that the monarchs would be Protestant. As a result, a German prince who could speak very little English became the British king, George I (r. 1714–27).

Large states and imperial systems dominated politics in the world at the beginning of the eighteenth century. It is a time both of attempted consolidation of centralized state power and of transformation of the very nature of the systems themselves. States in each of the world regions developed distinctive and diverse ways of rule while, at the same time, becoming more closely involved in broader global relations with other peoples and societies.

The world of politics was still a world of separate states at the beginning of the eighteenth century, but merchants and traders increasingly confirmed Roger North's vision of the world of trade "as one nation or people." The global networks of economic life changed the ways peoples interacted around the world. The networks themselves changed as businesses adopted new styles of organization. New products transformed the lives of rich and poor alike. While these transformations brought prosperity to many, the destruction caused by the slave trade and other ways of exploiting people show that the economic transformations had some high costs.

Adventurers and individual entrepreneurs were the key elements in earlier long distance trade. In the sixteenth century, the new global networks were informal and in many ways continued the older patterns of trade diasporas consisting of groups of traders living in different cities and regions, tied together by their economic enterprises and family or ethnic ties.[19] Much of the interregional trade in regions like the Indian and Atlantic Ocean basins and the old caravan routes of central Asia and the Sahara was controlled by such diasporas based in networks of trading posts scattered around the regions. The Portuguese attempted to turn the trading posts that they established in the Indian and Atlantic Ocean basins into a more centrally controlled maritime empire but by the end of the seventeenth century they were being replaced by other powers in those regions.

The new economic powers of the seventeenth century set important patterns for interregional economic relations, especially in the trade regions of Asia and Africa. The older patterns of interaction involved cooperation (and competition) among groups of small, independent companies as they operated in the networks of cities and trading posts. The new pattern was the formation of larger, more centrally controlled companies that also could mobilize military forces. Roger North's family was involved in an early venture of this type, the Amazon Company, whose royal charter was issued in 1619 to the "Governor and companie of nobleman and gentlemen of the Cittie of London: adventurers in and about the river of the Amazons."[20]

The early companies of "adventurers" were soon displaced by major monopolistic trading companies that had state support. The archetype of this new structure was the Dutch East India Company, the Vereenigde Oostindische Compagnie (VOC), which received its charter from the Dutch government in 1602. By the beginning of the eighteenth century, the VOC was joined by a host of similar companies, with the British East India Company (BEIC) emerging as the most powerful. These companies were not simply trading companies. Their leadership included many of the most powerful politicians of the day. For example, when competing British companies were joined together in the United Company of Merchants Trading to the East Indies in 1709, its subsequent chairmen included people like Charles Peers, who was Lord Mayor of London. In the areas of their commercial enterprise, the companies were major administrative structures with their own military forces, and in the early decades of the eighteenth century they came to administer and control territories as well as engage in commerce. The VOC, working through local rulers who became agents of the company as well as administering some areas directly, emerged as a major "state" in the islands of Southeast Asia. Similarly, the BEIC assumed many of the functions of the state as it began to administer territories in India in the name of the Mughal sultans. The Anglo-French struggle for dominance in India was primarily a conflict between the BEIC and the French East India Company (Compagnie des Indes Orientales). Similar corporate rivalries shaped world trade patterns in Africa and the Caribbean.

Much of the companies' profits rested on new products that transformed global trade in the centuries following the integration of the Western Hemisphere into the world economy. The companies played an important role in what some have called the "Hot Drinks Revolution" based on the growing popularity of coffee, tea, and chocolate, especially

The British East India Company coat of arms with its royal lions and flags provides an image of the Company as a state operating, as its motto states, "under the auspices of the sovereign and senate of England." By the end of the eighteenth century, the Company provided the framework for expanding British power in South Asia. © The British Library Board

when consumed with sugar.[21] What had been elite luxury consumption items became staples of popular consumption.

By the eighteenth century, sugar was probably the most important commodity in global and interregional trade. The popular new beverages created demand for large amounts of sugar, and sugar by-products like molasses were used in other foods and beverages. Sugar production became a major industry in the global economy. Although there are many different kinds of sugar, sugar from cane rapidly became the dominant form.

The growing demand led to the further development of large-scale agricultural complexes with a distinctive form of organization: the plantation. Plantation sugar production was labor intensive and required large amounts of cheap labor. While earlier sugar production in the Mediterranean basin had involved coerced labor, it was not until the rapidly growing demand for sugar in the seventeenth century that slave labor became an essential part of the plantation production system. The close ties between enslaved labor and the operation of the plantation system was clearly described in 1713 by William Cleland, a Scottish business agent in the Caribbean. In considering the trade of the Sugar Colonies and the trade with Africa, he stated that "these Two Trades are like the Cause and the Effect, without one, the other cannot stand; that is, if the Colonies are not furnished with Negroes, they cannot make Sugar."[22]

The growth of the Atlantic slave trade is directly related to the demands of the sugar market. The result was the forced displacement of millions of people from Africa to work in the plantations of the Western Hemisphere. This major forced population movement brought African peoples and cultures to the Americas and significantly altered the course of history in their homelands as well.

The broader development of a global economy involved a wide range of products from many regions. The islands of Southeast Asia had long been involved in the transnational spice trade and, by the beginning of the eighteenth century, new products like sugar and coffee became a significant part of exports from Java. India established a major favorable balance of trade surplus with the rest of the world, especially benefitting from exports of cotton textiles to Europe and western Asia. Northern lands in Eurasia and North America were major exporters of furs. Food grains and timber products from many different regions added to the rapidly growing volume of trade. In economic terms, with the great expansion of interregional commerce, the world increasingly fit North's description of the one nation of the world of trade.

The important developments transforming economic and political life also affected religious beliefs and institutions. Tensions between institutional and individual expressions of faith are normal parts of religious history and they took distinctive forms in the major urban-agricultural societies during the early eighteenth century. The main traditions in these societies maintained continuity, with Christianity, Islam, Judaism, Hinduism, and the Confucian-Buddhist-Taoist synthesis in China remaining the major worldviews in Europe, the Middle East, India, and East Asia.

The dominant religious institutions and "orthodoxies" were challenged in a number of ways. Some of these challenges, like the movement of Dona Beatriz in Kongo, came from leaders promising a new age that would transcend the current institutions. Others taught that the mainstream traditions had departed from the pure fundamentals of the faith tradition. The interactions among the messianic visionaries, those advocating a return to basics, and the conservative preservers of tradition shape the dynamics of early eighteenth-century religious history. At the same time, some thinkers, especially in western Europe, began experimenting with new visions of the universe. They provided the basis for what came to be modern science. However, at the beginning of the eighteenth century, the new cosmologies were not seen as contradicting the main traditions of religion.

The early eighteenth century is not a time of major religious reformations or revolutions. However, in the major religious traditions, believers presented responses to grand medieval syntheses of doctrine and practice like the Christian theology of Thomas Aquinas, the neo-Confucianism of Zhu Xi, and the scholars who developed Islamic jurisprudence. Other movements worked to reshape the relationships between their religious traditions and the emerging political systems in their societies.

In China, the establishment of the new Qing dynasty in the middle of the seventeenth century had important consequences for the development of Confucian thought and belief. The Kangxi emperor, as a part of his policies of consolidating Qing rule, issued a "Sacred Edict" in 1670 that presented a summation of Confucian moral values. This Edict confirmed the dynasty's support for neo-Confucianism, the broad synthesis that is identified with the comprehensive teachings of the medieval scholar Zhu Xi (1130–1200). The emperor proclaimed, "If there are the same doctrines and customs all over the Empire, the Peaceful Age will again be seen in our day. Will it not be excellent?"[23] He also confirmed and strengthened the examination system for government officials.

This imperial reaffirmation of neo-Confucianism by the new dynasty was challenged by a significant group of scholars who developed an analytical methodology called "practicing evidential research" (*kaozheng*). The group is sometimes called the "School of Han Learning" because of its attempt to return to the ideas of the early Han dynasty. They worked to understand texts from before Zhu Xi's time in an effort better to understand the ideas of Confucius himself, rather than simply accepting the conclusions of the traditions of neo-Confucian interpretation. This approach was both a notable contribution to scholarship and a vehicle for criticizing the establishment scholars who were described by the seventeenth-century scholar Yen Yuan as "sitting majestically in their studies" while the true sages "all worked practically to bring about the right way in the world."[24] This effort was a challenge to existing thinking, demanding a return to the original sources.

The new methodology was also used to provide a critique of imperial authoritarianism. A seventeenth-century pioneer in the School of Han Learning compared the current rulers with the virtues of the early emperors, who spent their whole lives "working for the welfare of the people. . . . Anciently the people loved and supported their ruler. . . . Nowadays people resent and hate their ruler, regarding him as a thieving enemy."[25]

The neo-Confucian synthesis was both affirmed by Qing emperors and criticized by scholars like those in the School of Han Learning. Similarly, in terms of the relationships between Confucianism and the state, no one argued for the abolition of the imperial monarchy, and both the emperor and the scholars confirmed that Confucian values were the necessary foundation for the state. The debates dealt with how the Confucian tradition was to be understood.

The Muslim world at the beginning of the eighteenth century was more diverse than China and had no central political or religious institutions. Muslim majority societies existed not just in the Middle East but also in sub-Saharan Africa, southeastern and central Asia, and southern Europe. However, even with this great diversity, Muslims faced the general challenges of articulating and responding to the established doctrinal schools of jurisprudence and the mystical devotional traditions as well as continuing to define the relationship between the religious tradition and their political institutions.

Some Muslim states were long established, with recognized Islamic authority. The Ottoman Empire of Sultan Ahmad III was an imperial state with firmly established governmental institutions of mosques, schools, and hierarchies of religious scholars. Even in the time of violent revolt, as when Ahmad III was overthrown, the continuation of the empire as a Muslim state was not in question. Similarly, the states ruled by Muslim Khans in central Asia had deep roots for Islamic identity.

In some regions, however, the relations between the cosmopolitan orthodoxy of the multi-cultural global community (as that orthodoxy was presented in comprehensive teachings of scholars like Ahmad ibn Taymiyya) and the state were still being defined. Islam was a more recent arrival in sub-Saharan Africa and Southeast Asia. In societies on the frontiers of the Muslim world, rulers adopted Islam but often continued important pre-Islamic practices in the operation of the state. Movements to intensify the Islamization of these societies frequently clashed with these rulers. In West Africa, for example, movements of Islamic purification, sometimes proclaimed as jihads, began in the late seventeenth century in the regions of present-day Mauritania and Senegal. These movements succeeded in establishing a number of states throughout the region in the following century. In Southeast Asia, Muslim teachers interacted with rulers who often maintained courts reflecting Hindu and Buddhist political traditions. The results varied. In Java the old-style court traditions continued while in places like Aceh on Sumatra, a more explicitly Islamic sultanate was established. At the beginning of the eighteenth century, the foundations were laid, in both Africa and Southeast Asia, for the more activist tensions and jihads that would occur later in the century.

Two major Muslim states experienced significant religiously influential political changes in the early years of the eighteenth century. The Mughal Empire in its early days of expansion under Akbar (r. 1556–1605) followed a religiously inclusive policy in dealing with the politics of Muslim minority rule over a Hindu majority population. Those policies aroused a strong "back-to-basics" response from a major teacher, Ahmad Sirhindi (1564–1624), who asserted that during Akbar's reign, "the infidels forced pagan practices on this Muslim land, and Muslims were prevented from observing their religious commandments."[26] Sirhindi's purist-reformist perspective shaped the policies of Awrangzib, as he worked to establish a more exclusivist Islamic identity for his state. This effort took many forms, from restricting musical entertainment and dancers in the court to attempting to impose the traditional Muslim poll tax on non-Muslims. While these policies received the support of many Muslims in the Mughal political elite, they also aroused a response from Hindus that became a part of Indian religious turmoil at the beginning of the eighteenth century. The major threat to Awrangzib's rule at the end of his life came from Hindu warlords and local rulers.

The second Muslim state engaged in a major redefinition of the role of religion in politics was Iran. The Safavid dynasty conquered much of Iran by the early sixteenth century and established an imperial state with Twelver Shi'ism as its official state religion. Twelver Shi'ism is the tradition of most Shi'ites in the world. Adherents differ from the Sunni Muslim majority in believing that the Caliphs, who were the successors to the Prophet Muhammad as leaders of the Muslim community, were illegitimate and that the rightful rulers (with the title *Imām* in Shi'ī tradition) should have been Ali, the son-in-law of the Prophet, and his descendants. Twelver Shi'ism teaches that the twelfth Imam in this line of descendants will return after being in seclusion to establish God's rule. Throughout Islamic history, one of the recurrent themes has been Sunni–Shi'ī rivalry.

Shi'ī movements had relatively limited success in establishing states based on their political theology. The major Shi'ī theological syntheses presented by scholars like Nasr al-Din al-Tusi (1201–74) included a messianic vision of the political future that shaped Shi'ī political expectations in the eighteenth century. The twelfth in the line of rightful Imams is believed to have gone into divinely protected seclusion (in the tenth century CE), to return at the divinely appointed time for the establishment of God's rule on earth. In this context, the political role of the Shi'ī ulama (religious scholar-teachers) was to provide guidance to rulers who happen to be in power, while awaiting the return of the Imam. In the sixteenth century, the Safavid rulers created a religious establishment within this framework, granting them a substantial degree of economic and intellectual independence from the monarchy.

By the beginning of the eighteenth century, the Safavid state was approaching collapse. Its continuing wars with the newly expanding Russian Empire and its Sunni neighbors, the Ottoman and Afghan Empires, weakened the state and resulted in significant territorial losses. The last reigning Safavid shah, Sultan Husayn (r. 1694–1722) illustrates the increasing ineffectiveness of the rulers. He undertook self-glorifying and expensive construction projects and was so involved in the pleasures of the court festivities and the harem that a visitor said he "is quite careless of the welfare of the state."[27] A leading military commander stood up in the court at a major festival and told the shah "that he was an ignorant Prince, and that he would never know anything; and that in short he could not prevail on himself to serve him any longer."[28] In 1722 invading Afghan forces captured Isfahan, the Safavid capital, and the shah surrendered. In 1726 he was murdered by his Afghan captors and the dynasty, for all practical purposes, came to an end. These events

Nadir Shah of Iran met with the Mughal sultan, Muhammad Shah, in Delhi following the Iranian victory over Mughal forces in 1739. Nadir Shah is seated slightly higher than the Mughal ruler to indicate the Iranian ruler's dominance at that time. © RMN-Grand Palais/Art Resource, NY

opened the way for a Safavid heir to join with a strong military commander, Nadir Afshar, in order to preserve the dynastic state. However, in 1736, that soldier deposed the Safavid pretender and proclaimed himself as Nadir Shah.

The change of regime shifted control of the monarchy to military commanders, who allowed the ulama (religious scholar-teacher) and their schools and endowments to flourish. This development reflected the growing power of the ulama already in the final decades of Safavid rule. Under Sultan Husayn, one scholar, Muhammad Baqir al-Majlisi, emerged as a major person of power in the court. He was a puritanical reformer who strongly opposed Sunnis and the Islamic mystical traditions of Sufism. He brought together one of the largest collections of traditions about the sayings and teachings of the Prophet Muhammad and the Imams, as a way of getting to core basics of Shi'i faith. He translated much of his scholarship into Persian, saying that his goal was to make the traditions available "to the masses of believers . . . [in order to] give life to the hearts and spirits of the dead-hearted people."[29] After his death he was identified by many Shi'ites as the "renewer of the century," in line with the tradition reporting that the Prophet Muhammad said that God sends a renewer to community of believers each century.

The ulama emerged as a virtually independent force within Iranian society. However, crucial divisions among the scholars existed. Debates raged between ulama supporting greater application of rationalist analysis in the principles (*usul*) of jurisprudence and theology and those relying primarily on the reports of the sayings of the Imams (*akhbar*, traditions) as the source of religious and legal guidance. This conflict between the Usuliyyah and the Akhbariyyah (traditionists) goes back to the tenth century CE and scholars in the Usuliyyah school had long been the most influential. However, traditionist (Akhbariyyah) scholars tended to dominate the Iranian schools by the beginning of the eighteenth century. Although al-Majlisi attempted to define a middle way between the two schools, the conflict was a major part of intellectual and religious life in the Shi'i community throughout the eighteenth century.

In India, while back-to-basics sentiments dominated the politics of the Muslim ruling elite, significant developments shaped Hindu and other major faith traditions. Hindu responses to the restrictive policies of Awrangzeb and local Muslim rulers gave strength to revolts by Hindu leaders against Muslim rule. During the seventeenth century, Shivaji Bhonsle mobilized the Marathas in the central Deccan plateau. Through conquests and effective diplomacy, he established a large state utilizing traditional Hindu symbols of political authority. He and his successors engaged in long wars with the Mughals, and the Maratha Hindu empire was a major political force at the beginning of the eighteenth century.

In western Europe, the disastrous religious wars of the seventeenth century created a sense of caution regarding religion and politics. The religion of the state, especially as reflected in the religious identification of the ruler, was still important. The overthrow of Roman Catholic James II in Great Britain in 1688–89, and the establishment of the parliamentary monarchy under the rule of the Protestant co-monarchs William and Mary were shaped by popular opposition to having a Roman Catholic monarch ruling a Protestant majority country. When William and Mary, and their successor, Queen Anne, had no direct heirs, the Act of Settlement of 1701 made it mandatory that "all and every Person or Persons that then were or afterwards should be reconciled to or shall hold Communion with the See or Church of Rome or should professe the Popish Religion or marry a Papist should be excluded" from royal succession.[30] The emerging parliamentary system was definitely not a secular state. Similarly, relations between Catholic monarchs and the papacy continued to be a significant part of the emerging system of inter-state relations in Europe.

At the beginning of the eighteenth century, Catholic-Protestant competition continued to shape broader political and social policies. However, in theological and intellectual terms, the churches and religious traditions coming out of the Reformation era faced internal divisions as reformers and visionaries sought to reshape the major institutions. These reformist movements took many forms. Some believed that the great religious mission was to prepare for the coming of a divinely guided new age, while others advocated a reaffirmation of what they saw as the fundamentals of the faith tradition in calls for "back-to-basics" renewal of existing institutions.

In Catholic Christendom, the response to the Reformation included the establishment of a major organization, the Society of Jesus (Jesuits). By the beginning of the eighteenth century this religious order transformed religious education and expanded the missionary activity of the church around the world. Jesuits played a role in the intellectual life of the Qing imperial court of Kangxi in China and were active in Latin America and South and Southeast Asia. In Europe they represented institutional renewal and changed much in how the Roman Catholic Church worked with the states of the time.

The Jesuits were active in a number of theological disputes. They strongly opposed Jansenism, a theological movement initially defined by Cornelius Jansen in the seventeenth century that gained a large following in France by the end of that century. Jansenism emphasized doctrines of predestination and original sin, and Roman Catholic opponents accused Jansenists of being Calvinist, following the teachings of John Calvin, the Reformation leader who stressed those doctrines. Jansenism was an influential "back-to-basics" reform movement, calling for a return to what they interpreted as the true teachings of the early Christian thinker Augustine of Hippo. Jansenism attracted many followers among French intellectuals and clergy, and posed a threat to the theological authority of the church. Blaise Pascal, a French philosopher and mathematician, strongly supported Jansenism in his writings. Louis XIV viewed the movement as a threat to national unity and to his own authority. He supported the church's efforts to suppress the movement and destroyed the buildings of its most important center. After many debates, Pope Clement XI (r. 1700–1721) issued the papal bull *Unigenitus* in 1713 condemning Jansenist teachings as "false, captious, evil-sounding, offensive to pious ears, scandalous, pernicious, rash, injurious to the Church and her practice, insulting not only to the Church but also the secular powers."[31] The theological and intellectual battles of the Reformation were not finished.

Non-Catholic Christians in western Europe also continued to engage in theological debates and created a broad spectrum of new movements. One of the most important of these movements was Pietism, another back-to-basics effort to reform religious life by emphasizing personal spiritual piety with the early Christian community as a model. The Pietists charged that the existing churches of the day lacked a sense of individual devotional life and did not have the sense of fellowship and community that was seen in the early Christian community.

The foundations of the movement are in the preaching and organization of a seventeenth-century German Lutheran minister, Philipp Jakob Spener, who organized small study groups for devotional and scriptural study. In a question-and-answer presentation he emphasized the need for each person to engage in Bible study: "Is it proper for all Christians diligently to read the Scriptures? Yes. Since they are the letter of the heavenly Father to all his children, no child of God can be excluded from them, but all have both the right and command to read them."[32] Spener's emphasis on Bible study by the individual was a foundation for the life of piety advocated by Pietists in the eighteenth century.

The Quakers (Society of Friends) similarly emphasized the importance of the individual religious experience but in the context of a vision of the coming new age. William Penn, in the new settlement of Quakers in North America in which Mary Pennell lived, described this individualism explicitly: "That which the people called *Quakers* lay down as a main fundamental in religion is this—*That God, through Christ, hath placed a principle in every man, to inform him of his duty, and to enable him to do it; and that those who live up to this principle are the people of God.*"[33] This approach to religious life was a serious challenge to the institutional churches in the eighteenth century.

Major Jewish communities in Europe and the Mediterranean region also experienced new age and reformist movements. Religious expectations that a new era of world history was about to begin led many Jews in those regions to follow Sabbatai Zevi, a Sephardic rabbi living in Smyrna (Izmir) in the Ottoman Empire, who proclaimed himself to be the expected Messiah in 1665. He appealed to the traditions that God would send an anointed one (messiah) to restore the kingdom of the Jews and establish God's rule on earth. He was soon arrested by the Ottoman civil authorities. Although his movement failed, messianic expectations among Jews in Europe and the Mediterranean region remained high at the beginning of the eighteenth century. Some people believed, in the words of Glückel of Hameln, a Jewish businesswoman in Germany, that "were we not so wicked, but truly pious from the bottom of our hearts, I am certain God would have mercy on us" and fulfill the promise of the Messiah.[34]

Calls for true piety from the depths of the heart instead of the legalism of the scholars had long been a part of Jewish devotional traditions and a person manifesting that special piety was called Hasid in Hebrew. In the early eighteenth century this tradition became more formally organized in a Jewish movement similar to Pietism, identified as Hasidism. The most important leader in this development was Israel ben Eliezer, who became known in the 1730s as Baal Shem Tov ("Master of the Holy Name") in recognition of his piety. In the emphasis on faith of the heart, he said, "There are two levels in the study of Torah, Torah of the mind and Torah of the heart. . . . I have come to reveal Torah as it extends to the heart."[35] The Hasidic movement provided an alternative to the frugal legalism of Talmudic Judaism and became very popular among poorer Jews. This populist piety provided the basis for creating distinctive Hasidic communities, especially at first in eastern Europe. Although major orthodox Jewish teachers opposed Hasidic teachings and attempted to suppress the movement, it became an established part of Jewish life in Europe.

The sixteenth and seventeenth centuries had brought about major institutional changes, as the Lutheran Reformation established churches with strong clerical hierarchies but no pope and the Calvinists developed communities defined by doctrine rather than institutional hierarchy. The Catholic Church of the Counter-Reformation similarly transformed the previous structures, creating new institutions, such as the Jesuits, that were outside of the hierarchy of bishops and nationally identified churches. These new institutional arrangements became the established religious institutional order by the early eighteenth century. Movements like the Jansenists, Pietists, and Quakers represent the diverse ways that opposition to the institutionalized churches were manifested in the visions of religious renewal and reform.

Possibly the most significant religious development in the West by the early eighteenth century was the beginning of new ways of conceptualizing and understanding the universe. During the seventeenth century, many intellectuals were reconceiving the understanding of the physical universe, providing the foundations for what came to be understood as modern science. By the early eighteenth century, many of these widely divergent ideas were being brought together in grand theories of how the universe operates. New methods of analysis emphasizing inductive reasoning and empirical investigation provided the basis for new conceptualizations and cosmologies, defining new modes of thinking. While important initiatives took place in many fields, the major disciplines were astronomy, physics, and mathematics.

Isaac Newton's work is viewed by many, including his contemporaries, as an important culmination of these developments. His most influential work, *Philosophiae Naturalis Principia Mathematica*, published in 1687, provided an explanation for the motions of all bodies in the universe using the concept of gravity. The secretary of the Academy of Sciences in Paris, Bernard Le Bovier de Fontenelle, wrote in his eulogy for Newton. "This book, in which the most profound Geometry serves for a basis to a new system of Philosophy, had not at first all the reputation which it deserved, and which it was afterwards to acquire."[36] However, by 1718, a popular essayist, Thomas Brereton, could say that the name of Newton and his most visible defender, Samuel Clarke, "carrys such a Vogue in the learn'd World, that every *English* Reader must be more or less preposses'd in his favour."[37] Newton's "new system of philosophy" came to dominate scientific thought in western Europe during the eighteenth century and remains an important element in modern scientific thought.

Most people did not see this new vision as an alternative to religion but rather as a more effective explanation of fundamentally religious issues. Samuel Clarke, in the dedication essay to the Princess of Wales for a volume on the debates over Newtonism, noted that some people entertain suspicions "that the Foundations of *Natural Religion* were in danger of being hurt by Sir Isaac Newton's philosophy" but affirmed that "the Foundations of Natural Religion had never been so deeply and so firmly laid, as in the Mathematical and Experimental Philosophy of That Great Man."[38] Alexander Pope, a poet and younger contemporary of Newton, captured this meaning in an often-quoted saying which he proposed as Newton's epitaph: "Nature and Nature's laws lay hid in night: God said, 'Let Newton Be!' and all was light."[39]

The world of Roger North, Sultan Ahmad, and Dona Beatriz was a world of increasingly cosmopolitan relations, recognizing diversity. Some were extensions of earlier developments and others marked important innovations. However, in political organizations, economic networks, and new visions of human religion, changes were altering the landscapes of human life.

CHAPTER 3

Monarchs, Trade Companies, and Revivalists

"The Star of the North" that is how Voltaire described Catherine the Great. A French ambassador to her court reported that this empress of Russia is a "passionate princess" who "seems to combine every kind of ambition in her person."[1] In the second half of the eighteenth century, Catherine the Great was one of the most prominent rulers in a time that has been called the "Age of Absolutism." She ruled from 1762 until her death in 1796, and established Russia as one of the great powers of Europe.

Catherine was a princess in a small German principality. Through the marital diplomacy of the time, she married Peter Ulrich of Holstein, the only surviving grandson of Peter the Great and the heir to the Russian monarchy. Her husband's short reign, in 1761–62, ended with a military coup that placed Catherine on the throne. She became popular and the dominant personality in the Russian imperial court. She corresponded with and read the works of French intellectuals like Voltaire and envisioned herself as the model enlightened despot. Following the reforms of Peter the Great and going beyond them, the Russian Empire of her time was clearly no longer medieval in its basic character. At the same time, Russian society was still pre-industrial, and its basic political structures were different from those institutions conceived of as fundamental to the modern state systems that emerged in the nineteenth and twentieth centuries.

The empress worked to limit the power of the landed aristocracy and the established Orthodox Church as she strengthened the central administrative system. Catherine's policies were similar to those followed by rulers in the other major states of the era, as those states became increasingly centralized with more effective bureaucracies. In general the most effective organizing principle was dynastic monarchies of varying types. While in some regions, the subject peoples had a sense of communal-cultural identity that was associated with the dynastic state, these eighteenth-century states were not "nation-states" in a modern sense of the identification of the state with the culture and history of

The coronation of Catherine the Great, in 1762, as Empress of Russia confirmed her control of the central government after a time of political divisions. The splendor of her court impressed both Russian notables and foreign diplomats and supported her efforts to create a strong central state. Rare Book Division, The New York Public Library. "Koronovanie Imperatritsy Ekateriny II," The New York Public Library Digital Collections. https://digitalcollections.nypl.org/items/510d47e0-0e0e-a3d9-e040-e00a18064a99

the people. In these centralized monarchies, the people were seen as, and saw themselves as, loyal subjects of the rulers. The concepts of citizenship had limited if any influence. These monarchical institutions have a special eighteenth-century character.

This character of being neither medieval nor modern was seen in the economic and religious spheres of life as well as the political. The development of the porcelain industry in China during the eighteenth century, as reflected in the career of Tang Ying, the administrator of the major Chinese imperial porcelain-pottery production facility, demonstrates the evolution of global economic networks.

Tang Ying was the imperial supervisor of the great porcelain production center in Jingdezhen in south-central China from 1728 to 1756. A Chinese description of the pottery industry from the time affirmed that he "was deeply versed in the veins of the earth and the nature of fire. He selected with care all the materials and everything he touched was fine, lustrous, and wholly without spot."[2] He was commissioned by the Qianlong emperor to write a commentary to accompany a set of

20 paintings describing the production of porcelain. This account presents a remarkable portrait of the manufacturing process for porcelain in eighteenth-century China.

A contemporary wrote, "When alone he [Tang Ying] communed with flower and fruit and took them to his heart, his dragon jars and his Chün ware vessels, reverting to the methods of the past, recovered their old perfection, while his 'cock-kingfisher' and his 'rose' excelled the marvels of the present."[3] Tang Ying's artistic talent illustrates the combination of tradition with innovation that characterized Chinese porcelain manufacture over the centuries. The "dragon jars" had been the mainstay of medieval Chinese porcelain production, while the new rose-colored enamels, called *famille rose* ("Pink Family") by Europeans, were the product of innovative experimentation.

Famille rose porcelain is a reflection of the dynamics of eighteenth-century trade and economics. Chinese porcelain specialists developed a distinctive color palette with colors like *famille rose* for their products by combining new glass production technologies and porcelain colors that were being developed in Europe with important Chinese innovations in ways of creating colors and methods of porcelain production. Porcelain in *famille rose* patterns was very popular in Europe. Sometimes Europeans would redesign Chinese patterns and send requests back to China for their production, reflecting the more advanced state of Chinese porcelain production at that time. Tang Ying and his production center were a crucial part of this globally interactive eighteenth-century network of trade and production.

Tang Ying supervised the operation of one of the largest manufacturing centers in the world. The production processes brought large numbers of specialists together in assembly-line methods for mass producing the porcelain for both domestic markets and export. The center was not a modern-style factory utilizing newly developed machines. Instead, the production process was labor-intensive, using many workers, each of whom had special skills. The differences between the established Chinese porcelain industry and the emerging industry in Europe, especially in England, reflect the differences and availability of labor in the two regions.

In the middle of the eighteenth century, China was probably the largest exporter of manufactured goods in the world, and porcelain was one of the key products in that trade. Like tea, coffee, and sugar, Chinese porcelain had been a luxury, but became a part of daily life in many areas, and was especially popular in Europe. Richard Steele, the English essayist, spoke about the passion of women for China (porcelain):

This Chinese baluster vase is in the famille-rose pattern that was popular in Europe in the eighteenth century. Cooperation between Chinese producers of porcelain and European consumers in developing distinctive patterns illustrates the integrated nature of trade networks. Art Resource, NY

"There are no inclinations in Women which surprise me more than their Passions for Chalk and *China*. The first of these Maladies wears out in a little time; but when a Woman is visited with the second, it generally takes Possession of her for Life. *China* Vessels are Play-things for Women of all Ages."[4] Responding to this enthusiastic market, Chinese producers developed products specially designed for the European consumers.

The large demand for porcelain, both for wealthy collectors and daily use in drinking the newly popular hot beverages like coffee, tea, and hot chocolate, inspired Europeans to try to develop porcelain that could be competitive with Chinese products. Europeans had some success early in the eighteenth century in discovering ways of making porcelain. In Saxony, luxury porcelain was already produced in Meissen and Dresden by the 1720s, but Chinese products still dominated the market in the middle decades of the century.

The global porcelain market reflects the more general economic situation. In the middle of the eighteenth century, the limited interregional trade of medieval times was replaced by substantial trade in a variety of goods. Economic developments in one region had significant impact on other regions. However, no single region—China, Europe, or India—dominated the networks of trade and economic exchange. In the porcelain industry, it was not until late in the century that the impact of Josiah Wedgwood's industrialization of pottery manufacture in Staffordshire, England, began to alter the general shape of the global market. It was not until that time that the "modern" patterns of Western European domination of economic interregional relations and economic production began to emerge.

Many of the most important religious movements of the mid-eighteenth century were similar in style to the work of Tang Ying: they re-shaped inherited traditions while developing vivid and new expressions of those traditions. Shah Wali Allah in South Asia engaged in this blending of traditional and new in his movement of Islamic renewal and reform. His vision and theology became part of the intellectual foundations of modern Muslim thought and many of the major modern Islamic movements in South Asia claim his heritage. At the same time, some of his most influential work involved reformulations of significant medieval positions. However, in his view, independent and informed thinking (*ijtihād*) that is not tied to a mandatory following of past precedent was necessary: *ijtihād* "in every age is obligatory (on the Muslim scholars) . . . [because] every age has its own countless peculiar problems, and cognizance of the Divine injunctions with regard to them is essential."[5] He was neither a self-conscious preserver of medieval consensus nor a self-identified proclaimer of a new era in human history. He saw himself as a necessary reformer and renewer of Islamic faith and society in the context of the "peculiar problems" of his time.

In the middle of the eighteenth century, the Mughal Empire was disintegrating. The harsh reign of Awrangzib left a legacy of both divisions among the Muslim ruling elite and the rise of major non-Muslim groups with significant military power. Shah Wali Allah did not create an organization of his own; instead he worked with leaders of mystical Sufi brotherhoods and regional Muslim military commanders to recreate a sense of Muslim political unity. As a part of this, he preached against religious syncretism which integrated non-Muslim practices into Muslim life, advocating a "back-to-basics" position in the tradition of the earlier reformer, Ahmad Sirhindi.

In theological and intellectual terms, Wali Allah redefined the relationship between the study of Islamic jurisprudence (*fiqh*) and the understanding of the contents of the Traditions of the Prophet Muhammad (*hadīth*). In legal analysis, he advocated an approach that he called *tatbiq*, meaning "to bring into alignment or to make congruent," which involved "looking beyond the surface features to the inner essence or the comprehensive principle underlying a particular issue."[6] He emphasized the importance of independent analysis rather than acceptance of inherited customs and precedents. This position calls for a return to the fundamentals that echoes such earlier eighteenth-century religious revivalists as the leaders of jihads in Africa and Southeast Asia and the Pietists in Europe.

Globalization in the mid-eighteenth century created challenges to previously relatively isolated peoples and cultures. Transnational economic enterprises and expansions of new imperial states confronted nomadic peoples and tribal and village societies around the globe. From Siberia to the plains of North America and the islands of the Pacific Ocean, indigenous peoples were subordinated or displaced and sometimes killed off. Conasatego, an Onondaga chief in the Iroquois confederation in North America, described the type of problems that tribal peoples had as they faced the expansion of the dominant urban societies around the world. He told British officials, "Your people daily settle in these lands [still controlled by the confederation], and spoil our hunting. . . . It is customary with us to make a present of skins whenever we renew our treaties. We are ashamed to offer our brethren so few, but your horses and cows have eaten the grass our deer used to feed on."[7]

The millennia-old struggles between hunters and farmers or the dangers of nomadic peoples conquering urban societies were replaced by a new historical dynamic of long-term destruction or absorption of hunters, farmers, and nomads by the major urban societies. Non-urban peoples and societies continued to be important parts of human life but the basic story of their histories was changed from a story of continuities to one of transformations and extinctions.

Globalization in the eighteenth-century pattern did not involve imposition of the power of one of the major societies on the rest of the world. In the new global context of the eighteenth century, no single society dominated the vast networks of interactions among these societies. Instead, relationships among these urban societies reshaped the nature of the distinctive regional cultures within the context of truly global frameworks for activity. The new interconnected world basically brought an end to the historic competitions among the older ways of life, leaving city-based societies as the dominant form of social and economic organization in all parts of the globe. Although some hunting-gathering groups still existed in isolated areas, developments like the consolidation of Russian control in Siberia and Bantu-Dutch dominance over the San people in southern Africa represent the final culmination of the long historical competition between this earliest human way of life and later ways of organizing human life.

Small-scale agricultural communities were also under pressure. A change took place in the way agriculturalists lived. Rather than being independent farmers, they became "peasants" under the control of landlords and the politico-economic elites of their societies. The resistance of farmers to this exploitation was expressed over the centuries by peasant revolts, taking many different forms. The major peasant revolts in the eighteenth century were the last to significantly threaten the urban domination over rural peoples.

The rebellion led by Emelyan Pugachev in Russia during 1774–75 has been called the last of the great, old-style peasant revolts in Russia. Pugachev was one of the Cossacks, the farmers and horsemen living in semi-independent communities of the southern and eastern frontiers of the Russian Empire. The reforms of Catherine the Great had expanded the powers of the Russian aristocracy as landlords controlling the lives of the peasants. The economic exploitation of the peasants and the ruthless suppression of any opposition led to increased discontent that was mobilized by Pugachev. The goals he announced in his "imperial manifesto" directly address the popular grievances. He said that as ruler, "I will free all the peasants [from their serfdom] and exterminate the nobles down to the last man."[8] Through Catherine's reforms and autocratic rule, as an informed observer wrote, the "Princess had given much cause of offense to the greatest part of her subjects," and the revolt led by Pugachev became a "dreadful storm" that "threatened to subvert the throne of Catherine."[9]

One proclamation by Pugachev illustrates popular resentment over some of the cultural reforms supported by Catherine and Peter the Great. These changes included changes in ritual and theology in the Russian Eastern Orthodox Church that were opposed by a tradition that came to be called the Old Belief. There was also popular opposition to imposition of Western-style clothing and other customs that were viewed as part of the imperial policies of Westernization. Pugachev announced, "If God gives me power over the state, and when I have captured Moscow, I will order everyone to follow the Old Belief [the old Russian Orthodox practices] and then wear Russian clothes. I will forbid the shaving of the beard."[10] Even following serious military defeats, Pugachev was able to mobilize "swarms of kosacs [Cossacks] of kalmucs, of baschkirs and of peasants, whom the very name of liberty, and the desire of shaking off the yoke of oppressive masters, had induced to abandon their labours and resort to arms."[11] However, experienced troops who had been fighting the Ottomans in the Balkans became available following the end of the Russian-Ottoman war in 1774, and Pugachev was defeated by a new Russian imperial commander given special authority by the empress.

In the areas that remained outside of the control of the major urban societies, some of the smaller communities expanded into large chieftaincies. By mid-century, the major urban societies incorporated, sometimes by conquest and at other times by economic integration, many of the remaining small agricultural groups. The great chieftaincies in North America and the Pacific basin faced significant challenges and opportunities in the middle decades of the century.

The Iroquois confederation in North America participated actively in the wars between Britain and France. The North American manifestation of the Seven Years' War resulted in the fracturing of the Iroquois network of alliances. During the American Revolutionary War, the Iroquois sided with the British but they were subordinates rather than allies. British General John Burgoyne emphasized their weaker position in an address to Iroquois chiefs in 1777: "This war to you my friends is new; upon all former occasions, in taking the field, you held yourselves authorized to destroy wherever you came, because everywhere you found an enemy. The case is now very different," and he set forth rules of engagement that set limits on attacking European civilian settlers. The major chief present replied, "With one common assent, we promise

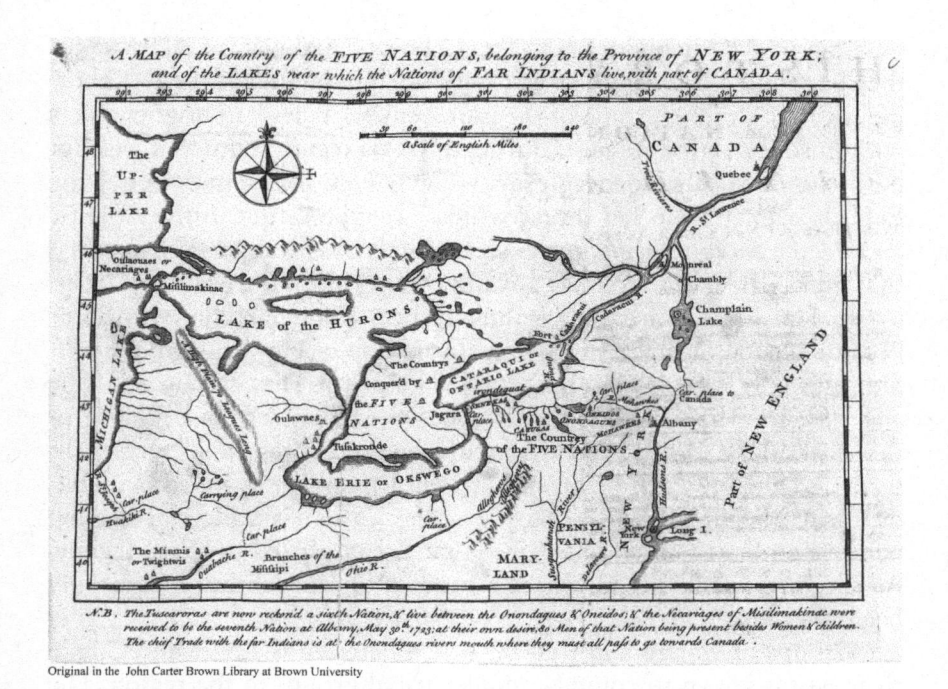

Original in the John Carter Brown Library at Brown University

This map identifies the large region controlled by the Iroquois confederation in the Great Lakes region of North America in the middle of the eighteenth century. The confederation lost control of much of this territory by the end of the century to expanding European imperial powers. Courtesy of the John Carter Brown Library

a constant obedience to all you have ordered, and all you shall order."[12] By the end of the century Iroquois territories were largely under European control. In the western part of the continent, major Native American groups such as the Apaches maintained some effective independence, but that was more the result of isolation and the weakness of their Spanish opponents than of their own effective power for resistance.

In the Pacific basin, the great chieftaincies in major clusters of islands continued to develop more consolidated power structures based on complex alliances of clans and kin relationships. In the middle of the eighteenth century, they still remained largely outside of the emerging global trade networks. In many areas, the older patterns of small chieftaincies in networks of cooperation and conflict continued. When Lewis de Bougainville, a French admiral who was the first Frenchman to lead a scientific expedition around the world, visited Tahiti, he reported, "Though the isle is divided into many little districts, each of which has its own master, yet there does not seem to be any civil war. . . . [However,] they are almost constantly at war with the inhabitants of the neighboring isles."[13] Although some of the island chieftaincies had brief contacts with European entrepreneurs during the seventeenth century, it was not until the more sustained enterprises of people like James Cook, the English seaman who led three voyages of exploration in the Atlantic and Pacific Ocean basins in the second half of the eighteenth century, that Europeans began to have any important role in the island societies.

In Hawaii, Cook met a young prince, Kamehameha, who later became the major figure in the transformation of Hawaii from the pattern of small chieftaincies into a unified kingdom. However, in 1789, he was described by Cook's ship surgeon, David Samwell, as a relative of the local ruler and of a "blackguard appearance," dressed in "an elegant feathered cloak, which he brought to sell."[14] Cook was killed in a conflict with some of the local warriors during this visit. He was dealing with a number of chieftains rather than a centralized political regime. At the time of Cook's death, the process of centralization was only beginning.

Groups of warriors in Central Africa between the Nile and Congo river basins began to conquer smaller tribal groups in the region. The Avungara leaders of the Azande (plural of Zande) established a powerful chieftaincy by 1700, and their control expanded during the following century. Previously distinctive groups were incorporated into an emerging Zande identity. This expanded chieftaincy provided the organization for control of a major region and for resistance to outside invaders, from the Egyptians in the nineteenth century to the British in the twentieth. Similarly, farther south, a new Luba state emerged that was, by the late eighteenth century, the largest kingdom south of the sultanates of the Sudanic regions of the sub-Saharan savanna. The Zande and Luba states were quite different in their organizations and administrative structures, reflecting the great diversity of political options in the middle of the eighteenth century.

European powers had little success in conquering any of the states in the coastal and sudanic regions of sub-Saharan Africa, except in the southern regions. The Portuguese had success earlier but by the eighteenth century they were driven out of the great trade cities of East Africa. The rising power in the eastern coastal region was the Sultanate of Oman in South Arabia. Oman created a powerful navy that was the basis of its East African/South Arabian empire. The success of the Omani state as a maritime power in the eastern Indian Ocean reflects the relative balance between local and European powers in the middle of the eighteenth century. The relations between local states and European commercial entrepreneurs in West Africa were similarly balanced, with kingdoms like the Ashanti maintaining independent power until well into the nineteenth century.

Muslim sultans, Chinese emperors, and European kings and queens led societies that were identified with different religious traditions. They enforced their political authority through distinctive institutions of military organization and administrative structures. As a result, the responses of states and organizations to the emerging global web of inter-societal relations were diverse, and often competitive. These interactions were not so much a clash of civilizations as they were the continuation of alternative solutions to globally common issues. China, India, Europe, and the Middle East all remained fundamentally urban societies but with new adaptations required by the conditions of the world of the eighteenth century.

Catherine the Great's policies of strengthening the central government reflected the broader efforts of rulers from Frederick II in Prussia and Joseph II in the Hapsburg Empire to the Mughal sultans in India and the Qianlong emperor in China. The new centralization frequently involved strengthening the efficiency of governmental administration by replacing hereditary overseers with a more professional bureaucracy. The core of the states usually continued to be a monarchical dynasty. Older local aristocracies were weakened or replaced by new central political elites that combined old nobilities with new merchants and professionals whose power was increased by the wealth created by the globalization of economic enterprise. A radical example of this replacement was when, following a series of military victories by the East India Company, the Mughal ruler, Shah Alam, proclaimed the Company to be his bureaucracy in the major Mughal province of Bengal. The mature eighteenth-century political system involved little or no sense of citizenship or political participation on the part of the majority of the population. Even in the parliamentary system of limited monarchy in Great Britain, the political class was very small and represented a power elite.

The development of gunpowder weaponry played a crucial role in defining the new states. The shift to musket-armed infantry and artillery as important elements in military power changed the balance of power in the states themselves. Landed nobles who provided the old-style cavalry lost at least some influence to the emerging professional officers in the new infantry corps. The Ottoman Empire was a pioneer in this shift when it established an elite musket-armed infantry corps, the Janissary Corps. This development reduced the influence of the rural civilian leaders in the Ottoman court. The guns of the new states were expensive and gave added strength to strong central governments because local notables could not afford the cost of a major gunpowder force. The greater financial and manpower resources of strong central governments enabled them to develop new style military forces that could greatly expand the areas under their control. As a result, some scholars have called the era from the fifteenth through the eighteenth century, the age of "gunpowder empires,"[15] with societies adopting the new technologies in different ways.

The core of this political style was the strong central state built around the continuing traditions of monarchy. The power of the gunpowder monarchs was qualitatively greater than the power available to medieval imperial and feudal rulers. Often the rulers, in fact, were remarkably cosmopolitan and not tied to the cultures of the peoples they ruled. Before Catherine the Great was empress of Russia, she was born a princess in a small north German state. She was chosen as the wife for the heir to the Russian throne, Peter III, who was himself part of the cosmopolitan royalty of the day. He was a German prince and a grand nephew of the king of Sweden as well as a grandson of Peter the Great. Before he was announced as heir to the Russian throne, he had been proclaimed the king of Finland and named heir to the Swedish throne by the Swedish parliament. Catherine the Great encouraged Russian thinkers and authors but the intellectual core of her court were European cosmopolitans of the Enlightenment.

Throughout the European state system, royalty was cosmopolitan in identity. Even the most nationally identified states like Great Britain did not expect the monarchs to be identified with local or national culture. At the beginning of the century, Parliament determined that a German (Hanoverian) prince, who became George I (r. 1714–27), would be the parliamentary monarch of Britain. The sister of George II (r. 1727–60), the Hanoverian king in the middle of the century, was the wife of the ruler of Prussia and his daughter married the king of Denmark.

Following the establishment of a competitive state system set in motion by the Treaties of Westphalia (1648), many of the major European wars were wars of dynastic competition for control of important monarchies. At the beginning of the eighteenth century, the War of the Spanish Succession (1701–14) brought the Hapsburgs and the Bourbon dynasty of Louis XIV into conflict over the throne of Spain. The Treaty of Utrecht at the end of the war brought an end to the wars of Louis XIV and established a balance of power among the major states. The next major European war was the War of the Polish Succession (1733–35), in which France, Russia, and Austria fought to control the Polish monarchy, with much of the fighting taking place in Italy between the French and the Austrians. This war set the stage for the partition of Poland and the end of even its formal independence by the end of the century. The third major dynastic war was the War of the Austrian Succession (1740–48), which was a precursor to the more global conflict of the Seven Years' War (1756–63), with Britain and France fighting for overseas possessions and Austria and Prussia competing for dominance in central Europe.

Dynastic rulers in most centralized states in other parts of the world were also non-"national," even when they recognized the value of the cultural traditions of those that they ruled. In the middle of the eighteenth century, China was in the midst of the long reign of the Qianlong emperor (1736–96). After a century of Qing rule, the Qianlong emperor remembered that his grandfather, Kangxi, said, "What I fear . . . is that the children and grandchildren of later generations will abandon the Old Way, neglect shooting and riding, and enter into the Chinese Way."[16] However, the emperor balanced the necessity of maintaining the clear identity of the "Manchu" ruling elite on which his power depended with the encouragement of the Han Chinese bureaucratic elite and administrative traditions. Nevertheless, in language and domestic custom, the Qing dynasty was culturally distinct from the people it ruled.

Rulers of the major Muslim gunpowder states also retained cultural identities distinct from most of their subjects. The Ottoman dynasty was descended from a small group of Turkish-speaking warriors who established control of territories on the Byzantine-Islamic frontier in Anatolia. Their conquests made them rulers of large Christian populations in the Balkans and non-Turkish Muslims, especially Arabs, in the Middle East. Within this diverse empire, they maintained a distinct way of life. Military and administrative leaders were educated in official schools, providing a separate base for the governing officials. Ottoman court language developed as an ornate literary language fitting for court ritual. These institutions made it possible for the system to integrate new groups into the court elite by education and acculturation. The most important group to be integrated in this way was non-Muslim subjects who, as children, were taken as tribute and then became essential parts of the Ottoman military and bureaucratic institutions. This development also emphasized the separateness of the rulers from the ruled.

In South Asia, the majority of the subjects of the Mughal sultans were non-Muslim, and over the centuries the Muslim political elite developed its own language, Urdu. By the middle of the eighteenth century,

Mughal sultans increased the foreign nature of their imperial administration by outsourcing management of major areas like Bengal to the British East India Company.

Cosmopolitan rather than "national" monarchy was a key to the success of most of the large states of the mid-eighteenth century. Catherine the Great, for example, consciously spoke of the diversity of her domain and the need to recognize that character, in instructions to a law code commission in 1767: "In such a State as *Ours*, which extends its Sovereignty over so many different nations, to forbid, or not to allow them to profess *different Modes* of religion, would greatly endanger the Peace and Security of its Citizens."[17]

The Ottoman Empire permitted religious diversity and non-Muslim religious communities had some administrative autonomy within the political system. The Ottoman identity of the ruling elite was not ethnic. Many of the most powerful officials were legally slaves who were conscripted from non-Muslim communities and then trained in the government schools. In China, although Han Chinese culture dominated life in the public sphere, Han identity did not constitute a national identity for the subjects of the emperor. In India, even the exclusivist policies of Awrangzib did not end the involvement of Hindu and Sikh princes in the state. Cosmopolitan monarchy was the dominant form of large state rule.

Major European states also were primarily structured in this mid-eighteenth-century style of multi-ethnic, centralized dynastic polities. Even though French was the cosmopolitan language of courts and intellectual elites throughout Europe, in France many of the subjects of the king continued to speak local identity languages. At the beginning of the century, Britain had formalized this pluralism in the definition of the monarchy itself. The state was defined as the Kingdom of Great Britain in 1707, bringing together three distinct societies, England, Wales, and Scotland.

The British colonies in North America provided a different diversity and conflict, between overseas colonial settlers and the central government. Cotton Mather, a prominent preacher in Massachusetts, issued a complaint about "the Present Deplorable State of New-England" in 1707,[18] reflecting the efforts of the government in London to control colonial affairs more directly. In 1692, a number of the colonies in New England were brought together in the Royal Colony of Massachusetts. Before that time, Mather said that the "Inhabitants of *New-England* had for many Years . . . Enjoy'd the Liberty and Property of as Free and Easy a *Charter* as a People could Desire."[19] However, the rule by the royal governors in the new regime limited the freedom of action of the leaders of the colonists. Mather reported that James Dudley, the royal governor appointed in 1702, told the people, "in open Council," that *"the People in* New-England *were all Slaves"* and that *"they must not think the Privileges of* Englishmen *would follow them to the end of the World."*[20] The new settlement societies came increasingly into competition and conflict with the metropolitan centers in Britain, and ultimately declared their independence from Europe.

In regions of the Western Hemisphere ruled by Spain and Portugal, the Europeans were the ruling elite in a society that by the middle of the eighteenth century contained significant numbers of newly enslaved peoples from Africa to work in the expanding plantation economy, a growing population of *mestizos* (people of mixed European and Native American ancestry), and the large Native American population who descended from the rulers and subjects of the great states that existed before the arrival of the Europeans. Although this diverse population produced some movements of opposition to imperial rule, the major political division was within the ruling elite itself, between the creole aristocracy of descendants of early immigrants and the *peninsulares*, officials who came directly from the Iberian Peninsula. In a special report to the royal ministry in Spain, Don Jorge Juan and Don Antonio de Ulloa reported in 1749 that "cities and towns have become theaters of disunion and continuous bickering between Spaniards and creoles. . . . In Peru it is enough to be a European or chapetón to declare oneself immediately against creoles. To be born in the Indies is sufficient for one to hate Europeans."[21] Attempts by the Spanish Bourbon dynasty, which had come to power in the War of the Spanish Succession, to establish more effective central control increased the tensions in these colonies.

The eighteenth-century political systems were the products of the distinctive conditions of the time. Stronger central states led by dynastic monarchies were the core of this political world. The great urban societies continued to be balanced in their political power. However, the peoples of the world interacted with each other more intensively as the great global networks of trade and power politics developed.

"Nature seems to have taken a particular Care to disseminate her Blessings among the different Regions of the World, with an Eye to this mutual Intercourse and Traffick among Mankind, that the Natives of the several Parts of the Globe might have a kind of Dependence upon one another, and be united together by their common Interest."[22] Spectator, the journalistic observer created by the eighteenth-century essayists Joseph Addison and Richard Steele, presented this picture of the global economy while visiting the Royal Exchange in London. He listed many of the products involved in this traffic: "The Food often grows in one Country, the Sauce in another. . . . The Infusion of a China plant [tea] sweetened with the Pith of an Indian Cane [sugar]. . . . Our Rooms are filled with Pyramids of China, and adorn'd with the Workmanship of Japan: Our Morning's Draught [coffee] comes to us from the remotest Corners of the Earth."[23] This catalog of products and trade reflects three developments in the mid-eighteenth century: the increase in trade in important consumer items like porcelain, coffee, and sugar, the expansion of large-scale production facilities for those products, especially the expansion of large slave-based agricultural enterprises, and the evolution of the great trading companies, whose activities made the trade and production possible.

A description of the activities of the Dutch trading company reported that the "China Trade was always looked on to be the richest of all Asia, on account of the Value and great Quantities of Merchandize transported thence."[24] The great porcelain center in Jingdezhen supervised by Tang Ying continued to develop new products for the European market. The seventeenth-century porcelain trade had been dominated by blue and white ware but by the middle of the eighteenth century a broad range of colors, as in the *famille rose* export porcelains, were used. By the 1740s, the production of planned table services of matched pieces of porcelain added to the "pyramids of china" in Europe. The expansion of the porcelain trade was one part of the broader increases in trade in other consumer products.

By the middle of the eighteenth century, entrepreneurs grew important consumer products like coffee in many places around the world. Although originally most coffee was grown in Yemen, an agent of the Dutch East India Company began growing coffee in Java in 1707, and Java rapidly became a major exporter. By 1733 a catalog of "drugs" from London noted that while coffee originated in "the *Grand Seignior* [Ottoman Sultan]'s Dominions . . . the best comes now from the East Indies . . . [and] great Quantities are yearly imported from both parts."[25] Other regions soon became additional important sources. In the 1720s French agents began to grow coffee in the Caribbean and coffee cultivation began in Brazil later in the century.

In Latin America and the Caribbean, coffee became a major element in plantation economies built on extensive use of enslaved peoples from Africa. The French colony of Saint Domingue (now Haiti) became the world's largest producer by 1789. In Yemen and then in Southeast Asia, coffee was usually grown by small farmers on hillsides and then collected by merchants who would bring it into the trade networks. This development gave new importance to rural landowners who grew the coffee and the commercial agents who organized the trade, and weakened the authority of the traditional rulers. Whether through the creation of slave-based plantation economies or the emergence of new entrepreneurial classes, the expansion of coffee production, and other cash crops, changed the nature of political and social structures in many parts of the world.

The Minangkabau region of Sumatra, for example, had already begun to be integrated into the global economy in the seventeenth century because of the production of gold in the area. Minangkabau gold was an essential element in the developing VOC trade networks and gave strength to local monarchs in Sumatra. However, as the gold supply became exhausted in the eighteenth century, coffee emerged as a vital product in the changing trade patterns. The shift from gold to coffee resulted in a weakening of the old traditional monarchies and a strengthening of the Muslim merchants who managed the coffee trade. Similar shifts in power relations took place in other areas where coffee production gave wealth to new groups.

The new plantation economies required large numbers of inexpensive laborers. The result was a rapid expansion of the slave trade. The great slave plantations were created by the post-medieval global trade networks and were a major form of non-industrial production. The enslavement of large numbers of people in sub-Saharan Africa transformed societies there, bringing new entrepreneurs with armies, both African and European, into positions of control. Local African rulers traded slaves for large numbers of guns. In England, Lord Shelburne reported in 1765 that Birmingham engaged in "gunmaking to a prodigious amount for exportation . . . [and] send annually above a hundred and fifty thousand to the coast of Africa."[26] The result was the emergence of African military aristocracies with the capacity to conquer neighboring states. States in the eastern Niger delta, like Bonny, were among the new kingdoms that replaced older trading city-states. In other parts of the Atlantic world, Africans became important elements in societies throughout North and South America. This coerced movement of 10 to 15 million people created a cultural and demographic diaspora that became a significant element in societies in the southern English colonies in North America, the Caribbean, and South America.

By the middle of the eighteenth century, many of the smaller trading companies disappeared, as the major companies like the British East India Company (EIC), the Dutch East India Company (VOC), and the

French East India Company dominated global trade. Although these companies began as commercial trading enterprises, by the middle of the eighteenth century, the largest companies began to become more state-like in their positions around the world.

In India, the three major companies became rivals, working with local rulers and the Mughal court to gain control of markets and territories. By the 1740s, the companies' commercial rivalries became military conflicts as the companies joined with regional rulers in local wars for control of territories. Conflicts between the British and French companies also reflected the wars in Europe at the time The French gained some victories over the British in the 1740s during the War of the Austrian Succession, but British campaigns during the Seven Years' War (1756–63), culminating in the victory over the French at Pondicherry in 1761, brought an end to effective French power in India. Under the leadership of Robert Clive, an effective but controversial company administrator and military commander, the EIC consolidated power in India by becoming a major part of the Mughal governmental system. In the Treaty of Allahabad (1765) between the Company and the sultan, the EIC gained responsibility for civil, judicial, and financial administration in Bengal, the richest province in the Mughal state.

In much of India, the EIC was no longer simply the major trading company; it was also the de facto state. However, the Company-as-state was ineffective and corrupt. Robert Clive's successor as governor of Bengal, Harry Verelst, writing in 1772 after his governorship had ended, clearly defined the problems of this hybrid administration: "Unacquainted with the genius or manners of the inhabitants, their laws, or the power of their magistrates, the English were little qualified for the task of government. How could we make the sordid interests of the trader consistent with that unbiased integrity, that candid humane exercise of power, which must reconcile the natives to a new dominion? . . . The delegates of a company, possessing no right of legislation, might indeed have overturned the then subsisting government, but never could have substituted any other in its room."[27]

The chartered trading company as a semi-state may have been, as Verelst says, "little qualified for the task of government." Like the large plantation system, the company-state was a new creation emerging out of the contexts of increasing global interactions and the special conditions of the time. These major companies had modern descendants, among them Cecil Rhodes' British South Africa Company, but the later companies had to work with governmental institutions like the Colonial Office in Britain, which was established in 1854, rather than the more informal and political controls governing the companies in the eighteenth century.

The trading companies of the eighteenth-century style disappeared or were drastically reorganized by the end of the century. Most of the smaller companies were gone by the final quarter of the century and the two largest ones were soon to follow. The various "East Indies" and "West Indies" companies either were dissolved or taken over by the emerging centralizing states. In the case of the EIC, its ineffectiveness and corruption in provincial administration created protest in London. This situation opened way for the central government to begin to take control of the company. The first major step in this process was the Regulating Act of 1773, which centralized control of Company affairs in India and began to establish procedures for oversight of Company affairs by the Government in London.

A key figure in the ending of the era of freewheeling entrepreneurs was Lord North, Frederick North, who worked as an ally of George III in strengthening the role of the king in British politics. Lord North's family history illustrates the evolution of international commercial enterprise. An ancestor at the beginning of the seventeenth century was one of the "companie of noblemen and gentlemen of the Cittie of London" who were identified in their operating Charter as "adventurers in and about the river of the Amazons"[28] working to establish an agricultural plantation. The brothers of Francis North, his great-grandfather, were active investors in the later, better-organized trading companies with interests throughout the world at the end of the seventeenth and beginning of the eighteenth centuries. By the time of Frederick North, the age of the great trading companies was passing. Lord North, as prime minister, worked to provide governmental regulation, from London, of the activities of the Company through laws like the Regulating Act of 1773. His policies strengthened the processes of transition to the modern empire of the nineteenth century.

The French company endured major losses of market and territories to the British in India and experienced other financial problems. King Louis XVI ordered the Company to transfer its assets to the French state in 1770. The king formed a successor company in 1785, but it was dissolved in the aftermath of the French Revolution. The Dutch VOC became a major company-state administering a vast territory in the islands of Southeast Asia, and had problems similar to the British EIC. Profiteering entrepreneurs and corruption undermined the effectiveness of VOC control. The Anglo-Dutch War of 1780–84 resulted in the destruction of the VOC fleet, and efforts to restore its profitability failed.

The company was nationalized by the new Batavian Republic created in the aftermath of the French Revolution in the Netherlands.

Some significant religious debates in the middle of the eighteenth century involved defining the methods for determining authoritative interpretations of religious traditions. In China, the scholar Dai Zhen continued and expanded the critique of the neo-Confucian orthodoxy by the School of Han Learning, emphasizing the importance of studying the early Confucian classics rather than relying on later interpretations. Among Muslim Shi'i scholars, the debates between advocates of Usuliyyah (analysis of the basic principles) and Akhbariyyah (reliance on traditions of the Imams) continued. During the second half of the century, Aqa Muhammad Baqir al-Bihbahani established the dominance of the Usuliyyah approach, which emphasized the authority of the scholars qualified to interpret legal fundamentals. This development strengthened the independence of the ulama from the monarchy in Shi'ite Iran by making them the final authorities on legal matters.

Many highly visible religious leaders stepped forward to proclaim the need for reform and to present programs for the revitalization of their faith traditions. Like activists earlier in the century, the "renewers" were interacting with long-established institutions and working to reformulate or transcend those medieval frameworks in their traditions. What makes these reformers distinctive is the increasingly cosmopolitan nature of the networks of believers and the changing nature of the relationships between religion and politics in the major global societies. While these reform movements often called for purification of religious belief and practice in efforts to get "back-to-basics," this emphasis on core values of particular traditions was often cosmopolitan in mode, responding to new global interactions of peoples and cultures.

Shah Wali Allah, the great eighteenth-century South Asian Muslim scholar, reminded Muslims of the well-known saying of the Prophet Muhammad: "God will send to His community at the head of every century one who will renew its religion."[29] The figure of the divinely promised renewer or *mujaddid* is an important part of the Sunni Muslim theology of reform in the contexts of continuing historical change. Shah Wali Allah identified himself as this special reformer for his century. He lived in a time when the Mughal political order in South Asia was disintegrating. He died in the year before the EIC took control of the administration of Bengal, as the triumphant company became a dominant element in the changing Mughal system. In this troubled time, Wali Allah worked to support Muslim commanders who appeared as possible sources of stability within a framework of renewed Islam, but he did not establish his own independent organization as a political alternative.

Wali Allah concentrated his efforts, instead, on creating a theological and legal perspective that could provide a basis for unifying the many different sects and schools that had developed within Islam. In his major work defining this synthesis, he described his approach and goal: "You will find me—when the paths broke them up into branches and schools, and inclinations and preferences divided them—persevering in the evident, main, way and affirming the firm middle of the road."[30] In developing this middle-way for renewal, the central discipline is the study of *hadīth*—the accounts of the words and actions of the Prophet Muhammad. He argues "that the main topic in the fields of sciences of certainty (*ʿulūm yaqīniyya*) and their chief element, the basis of the religious disciplines and their foundation, is the discipline of hadith reports. . . . The one who follows them and keeps them in mind is rightly-directed and guided."[31]

Reformers throughout the Muslim world frequently presented their reform programs in terms of Hadith-based revivalism. This approach was a methodology that could reject existing customs and institutions, using the practices of the early Muslim community as a model. The practices of the "pious ancestors" or *Salaf* in the first generation of Muslims were the model for good Muslims. This "salafiyya" approach usually advocated the exercise of independent informed analysis of the sources rather than simply accepting the conclusions of previous scholars. In this way, the general principles of revelation could be adapted to particular circumstances of time and place since, as Wali Allah argued, "divine laws have preparatory circumstances and causes which particularize them, and which show certain of their possible applications to be more appropriate than others."[32]

One of the most long-lasting salafiyya-style movements was begun by the teachings and actions of Muhammad ibn Abd al-Wahhab in the central Arabian Peninsula. His activist opposition to existing practices inspired a local chieftain, Muhammad ibn Saʾud. The alliance between the teacher and chieftain resulted in the creation of a state based on a synthesis of tribal power politics and strict renewalist teachings. The modern kingdom of Saudi Arabia was built on the foundations laid by these two men and the king in the twenty-first century is a descendant of the founding chieftain. In contrast to Wali Allah, Ibn Abd al-Wahhab's renewalism was militant and combative, but still within the framework of hadith-based reforms. His teachings were in the "back-to-basics" mode, affirming, "We know definitively that whoever takes an issue disputed among the people back to the Book and the Sunnah [Traditions of the Prophet] shall find therein what shall resolve the issue."[33]

The movements in South Asia and Arabia had mid-century parallels in other parts of the Muslim world. The movements of Islamic purification that were proclaimed as jihads in West Africa early in the century continued their efforts for Islamization of societies. In Southeast Asia, Islamic renewalist movements were supported by the emerging entrepreneurial classes involved in the coffee trade, who provided financial support as well as numerous followers.

The mid-eighteenth century was also a time of major movements of religious renewal in the Christian world. Among non-Catholics in Europe, revivalist movements challenged the established Protestant churches and the accepted theological traditions based on the Protestant Reformation. These movements also challenged the continuing Catholic adherence to the teachings of medieval Catholic theologians. One of the most important new movements was Methodism, established in Great Britain by John Wesley, an almost exact contemporary of Muhammad ibn Abd al-Wahhab. His spiritual "method" of regular prayer, study, and enthusiastic evangelism challenged the hierarchical order of the Anglican state church. Although he did not intend to leave the Church of England, open air services and itinerant preachers reflected the spirit of what became, by the end of the century, a separate Christian denomination. His fundamental message was a challenge to current Church practice: "We look upon ourselves, not as the authors or ringleaders of a particular sect or party, . . . but as messengers of God to those who are Christians in name, but Heathens in heart and life, to call them back to that from which they are fallen, to real, genuine Christianity."[34] Wesley was inspired, in part, by the Pietists, and his approach was well-suited to the religious needs of the growing urban populations that tended to be ignored by the established institutional church. When the Methodist message was brought to the colonies in North America, it flourished, with circuit-riding ministries well suited to the colonial and frontier conditions.

Another religious renewal took place in the very different contexts of the world of Theravada Buddhism in South and Southeast Asia. Sri Lanka was a center of Buddhism from the very early centuries of the history of Buddhism. From the second century BCE, the monarchies of Sri Lanka were tied to Theravada Buddhism, a conservative Buddhist tradition that emphasized the sacredness of early texts of the teachings of the Buddha. Its community monastic tradition was central to its history. Over the centuries, monastic and dynastic lineages flourished and declined, with movements of revival regularly providing new energy and inspiration. In the middle of the eighteenth century, the island had been under attack from Portuguese and Dutch forces for two centuries. The kingdom of Kandy in the central highlands remained independent but coastal areas were under European control and there was pressure from Christian missionaries as well as European military forces.

Under these pressures, the monastic tradition had declined and it was reported by mid-century that there was only one monk left who still knew Pali, the language of the sacred texts. In that context, the senior monk Valivita Saranamkara began a revivalist movement that emphasized piety and knowledge of the scriptures. In the 1750s, he persuaded the ruler in Kandy to send a mission to Thailand in order to gain assistance in restoring the traditions of recognition of higher levels of authority for monastic leadership. The result was a visit to Sri Lanka by the leading monk in the flourishing Thai Buddhist kingdom, Upali Maha Thera. During this visit he performed hundreds of ordinations and Saranamkara became the Supreme Patriarch. This renewal of Theravada monasticism established the Siam Nikaya, which became the largest order of monks in the country. With its emphasis on a return to Pali scriptural literacy and the pure monastic tradition, the movement of Saranamkara is another variation of the renewalist movements of the mid-eighteenth century.

Throughout the world, movements of religious renewal interacted with religious establishments in ways that sometimes resulted in conflict. The movements of people like John Wesley were clearly different from state churches, and, even from the earlier Protestant Reformation. But Wesley was neither fighting against modernity nor promoting "modernism." His piety, like that of Wali Allah, Muhammad ibn Abd al-Wahhab, and Saranamkara, involved advocating renewal and reform of the conditions that they confronted in their time. Each of these leaders established foundations for what would become influential modern religious movements, as well as leading movements of renewal and reform within historic religious traditions.

Along with religious reform, thinkers in Western Europe continued to define new visions of nature and the cosmos. The new concepts and approaches of people like Newton were followed by activities in many fields like biology and chemistry as well as in physics. A new sense of skepticism and questioning of established institutions and beliefs characterized the thinking of intellectuals who shaped what has come to be called the Enlightenment. One of the most widely read critics was the French philosopher Voltaire, who viewed establishment Christianity as a system of intolerant superstitions. However, he framed his critique within the context of his times, comparing Christianity with other major religious traditions and reason rather than arguing within the framework of a new mode of knowledge. In his particular deism, he believed in a divinity who did not interfere directly in human affairs, and in a universe which, after its creation, operated in accord with natural laws. He satirically wrote, "If God did not exist, it would be necessary to invent him."[35] This approach is clearly a break from the conceptual world of medieval Europe, but he did not frame it in the terms of modern science either. He was an advocate of Newton's new worldview and he engaged in experiments, following the new approach to answering questions about natural phenomena. However, like Newton, his views were within the framework of natural religion and natural philosophy, with assumptions of divine design, rather than later modern concepts of empirical science. Voltaire's beliefs reflect the cosmopolitan viewpoint of an intellectual living in the time of the great dynastic monarchies—he was a favorite of Catherine of Russia—and before the development of the disciplines of "modern science."

In defining his natural philosophy, Newton wrote that "the main Business of natural Philosophy is to argue from Phaenomena without feigning Hypotheses, and to deduce Causes from Effects, till we come to the very first Cause, which certainly is not mechanical."[36] It was not until the final decades of the century that the distinctively modern disciplines with relatively narrowly defined subjects and experimental methodologies would begin to be defined.

One of the intellectual ancestors who shaped the biological science of Charles Darwin was Georges-Louis Leclerc, Comte de Buffon. His massive work, *Histoire naturelle, générale et particuliére* (1749–88), was a comprehensive and influential coverage of natural history, as understood in the eighteenth century. He is recognized as one of the pioneers laying the foundations for modern biology, but his intellectual discipline was "natural history," defined at the time as "that science which not only gives complete descriptions of natural productions in general, but also teaches the method of arranging them into Classes, Orders, Genera, and Species."[37] Like Voltaire, Buffon was an advocate of Newtonism as well as defining and expanding the field of study in what were to become the biological and zoological sciences. He is representative of eighteenth-century Western European thought, involved in reconceptualizing the understanding of nature but continuing to view nature within the cosmology of the age.

One of the major intellectuals of the time, Immanuel Kant, published an essay in 1784 entitled "Answering the Question: What is Enlightenment?" In this essay, Kant asserts that the motto of enlightenment is: "Have courage to use your own understanding." His essay is an advocacy of public use of reason but his definition remains associated with distinctive eighteenth-century institutions. He says, "If it is now asked, 'Do we presently live in an enlightened age?' the answer is, 'No, but we do live in an age of enlightenment.'" In defining what this means, he says that the obstacles to general enlightenment and human freedom from self-imposed immaturity are diminishing. He concludes this line of analysis by affirming that "this age is the age of enlightenment, the century of Frederick."[38] This thus identifies Enlightenment with one of the representatives of distinctive eighteenth-century dynastic monarchies, Frederick II of Prussia. Frederick was an active supporter of thinkers like Voltaire and the lack of censorship in Prussia under his rule provided freedom for Kant. Dynastic monarchies in the eighteenth century gave significant support to the development of Enlightenment thought. Like Frederick and Catherine, the Enlightenment is an important element in the changing history of the West (and the world) in the eighteenth century.

The world of Catherine the Great, Tang Ying, and Shah Wali Allah is a world of dynamic interactions and institutional change. The great dynastic monarchies, the pre-industrial intensification of global trade, and the movements of religious renewal in the major world religions all reflect the realities of the world in the middle of the eighteenth century. They also emphasize that although the major societies were no longer medieval, they were not yet modern.

CHAPTER 4

Shifting Balances
and Revolutions

A tombstone in Lancashire, England, identifies the burial plot of John and Ellen Hacking, "who invented the first carding engine that carded cotton for their neighbors and turned it by hand in Huncoat in 1772."[1] The small engine developed by this couple and used by Ellen Hacking was an essential part of the cotton manufacturing processes within homes that developed in late eighteenth-century England. The later cotton mills of Lancashire became almost iconic images of nineteenth-century industrial society, but in the late eighteenth century cotton cloth production by people like the Hackings was different from those large factories. Some historians consider the large cotton mills in Lancashire, England, as the starting point for the modern Industrial Revolution, whereas others emphasize the continuities with the older, small scale ways of producing cloth and other products. Both of these interpretations tend to ignore the distinctive character of global and local economies.

Cottage industries with production taking place in homes fit into the patterns of production and trade. Cotton production in households like the Hackings and networks of local weavers in India shaped the emergence of the cotton textile industry. Exports from India dominated global trade in cotton cloth early in the century. Governments encouraged cotton cloth production in Western Europe, providing legal protections from Indian imports by the middle of the century, even at times forbidding the wearing of popular Indian cloth like paisleys in public. However, the production of cotton cloth by the networks of weavers in India managed by merchants like the wealthy entrepreneur of Surat, Mulla Abdul Ghafur, was not significantly different from the methods of production in the cottages of Lancashire. Ellen Hacking increased the efficiency of existing methods rather than transforming the modes of production. That transformation only came at the end of the century with the shift to machine-based production and the beginnings of the large textile mills. This shift enabled British domination of the global textile trade.

Changes like the transition in the cotton industry from cottage industry to factory production were taking place in politics, religion, and world trade in general. Such changes in the late eighteenth century are especially visible in the political arena. The late eighteenth and early nineteenth centuries have often been called the Age of Revolutions. In virtually every region of the world, significant revolutions were harbingers of the modern politics that were to come in the nineteenth century. Revolutions are defined both by what they oppose and by what they advocate. Revolutionaries could advocate perfecting and correcting the existing institutions, defining their goals in terms of the eighteenth-century values, or they could offer a new vision, rejecting not just the existing institutions but even the ideal versions of those institutions.

The revolution in the British colonies in North America (1775–83) and the France Revolution (1789–99) set the historical framework for many of the revolutions of the era. They involved opposition to eighteenth-century conditions, but rapidly the revolutionaries began to define new institutions and ideals that shaped future modern states and societies. In the age of revolutions, the revolution in Haiti from 1791 to 1804 provides a clear picture of the broader revolutionary dynamics of the era by showing the interconnections between revolutions and the transition from opposition to the eighteenth-century institutions to advocacy of a new vision of society.

The eighteenth-century system of large plantations based on enslaved labor created conditions in many places for slave revolts against the harsh conditions under which they lived. By the late eighteenth century, the French colony of Saint-Domingue in the Caribbean (which became independent as the country of Haiti) produced around 40 percent of the sugar and 60 percent of the coffee consumed in Europe, making it probably the greatest wealth-producing European colony in the world. As many as 500,000 slaves (about 90 percent of the population) worked under extremely oppressive conditions. In economic terms, it was most profitable for plantation managers to cut expenses on food and medical care and work their slaves to death, replacing them by purchasing new slaves.[2]

Frequent revolts were brutally suppressed. Occasionally these revolts also involved freed slaves and *gens de couleur* ("people of color"), legally free people who were the children of slave owners and African women. These civil conflicts involving wealthy plantation owners, poorer whites, and *gens de couleur* intensified when French revolutionary pronouncements such as the Declaration of the Rights of Man and Citizen in 1789 proclaimed the liberty and equality of all citizens.

These developments provided the opportunity for a major slave revolt in 1791.

Initially most of the slaves involved appear to have viewed the revolt in the old-style terms of opposition to especially harsh conditions. However, leadership quickly passed to a group of men eventually led by Toussaint Louverture, a freed slave with managerial experience, who told the French Directory, the executive council leading the French revolutionary state in the late 1790s, that the French Revolution "changed my destiny as it changed that of the whole world."[3] Emancipation of enslaved people and the ending of legal slavery, rather than amelioration of specific bad conditions, quickly became central to the revolution.

A letter from leaders of the revolution to the colonial assembly clearly outlines the ideological transition from slave revolts against cruel plantation owners to a revolution framed by the emerging consciousness of the equality of all humans: "For too long we have borne your chains without thinking of shaking them off, but any authority which is not founded on virtue and humanity and which only tends to subject one's fellowman to slavery, must come to an end." The argument affirms natural equality: "What is the law that says that the black man must belong to and be the property of the white man? . . . We are your equals then, by natural right, and if nature pleases itself to diversify colors within the human race, it is not a crime to be born black nor an advantage to be white."[4]

These revolutionary words reflected the views of Toussaint Louverture, who began life within the eighteenth-century plantation system. He was the grandson of an African chieftain. His father was captured and brought to a plantation in Saint-Domingue, and Toussaint was born on that plantation. As a young man he worked effectively as a manager of livestock and held other administrative positions in a large plantation. He was freed while in his 30s. By the time of the revolution in 1791, he was a recognized leader and soon took command of armed forces in a strategically critical region. By 1801, he led the emerging political entity created by the alliance of the forces of the revolution and the remnants of French administration. The Constitution of 1801 defined the new state, setting the boundaries of its territory, and affirmed "In this territory, slaves cannot exist; servitude is permanently abolished. All men within it are born, live, and die free and French."[5]

The revolutionary government did not declare its independence until 1804, after the French had invaded Saint-Domingue and brought Toussaint to France, where he died in prison in 1803. The generals who succeeded Toussaint proclaimed the independence of their country, addressing the declaration of independence to the "people of Hayti." The French name of the country was rejected because, the declaration stated, "The French name still haunts our lands"[6] and people believed that the Taino, the pre-colonial inhabitants, had called the island "Haiti."

Although it had come into being as a revolutionary rejection of the established institutions of the eighteenth century, this new state continued eighteenth-century approaches. Jean-Jacques Dessalines and Henri Christophe, successors to Toussaint in leading the country, took the titles of emperor and king and worked to establish authoritarian monarchies. To restore the economy after the destruction of the revolution, both men attempted to restore the plantation system on the basis of forced labor, since the freed slaves did not voluntarily return to work in the plantations. However, these policies had limited success because of domestic political divisions and the oppressive nature of the restored plantation system. Haiti stood within the revolutionary tradition of the French Revolution without fully departing from the institutions of the eighteenth century.

Religious movements around the world tend to exhibit many of the same broad tendencies visible in the works of Ellen Hacking and Toussaint Louverture. In South Asia, the life and works of Ramanand Swami reflect a major transition taking place within the vast and diverse clusters of beliefs and rituals that came to be called Hinduism in the nineteenth century. Ramanand created an organization in the format that was standard for eighteenth-century South Asian religious practice, with autonomous local temples and teachers and diverse ritual traditions; it also served as the foundation for an organization established by one of his disciples that became an effective modern and later truly global devotional tradition.

The varied religious centers were associated with specific devotional traditions or *sampradaya*s. Among the most important of these *sampradaya*s are those identified with Shankara (ninth century), who provided a synthesis of philosophical and meditative traditions called Vedanta, and eleventh-century Ramanuja, who provided a broad framework for traditions of worship of a major Hindu divinity, Vishnu, defining Vaishnavism. Ramanand Swami became devoted to the tradition of Ramanuja after having followed the South Asian pattern of devotional piety and scholarship, traveling among the many holy sites in India, receiving guidance from a variety of teachers. He settled in Gujarat, where he established a Vaishnavite *sampradaya* that became a well-organized fellowship of teachers and followers. A young disciple who came to be known as Sahajanand Swami (and later Swaminarayan) joined the *sampradaya* in 1799. Ramanand saw spiritual power in this young man and in 1802 proclaimed him the leader of the fellowship. Ramanand died in that same year.

Under this leadership, the fellowship, now the Swaminarayan Sampradaya, grew rapidly. The group provided some sense of social order in Gujarat in the chaotic conditions of the decline of the Hindu state, led by military leaders from the Maratha ethnic group who had dominated the region since the time of their revolts against Awrangzib. Swaminarayan initiated programs of social reform through service projects for the poor. He advocated education for women and opposed the practice of *sati*, burning a widow on her husband's funeral pyre. His association combined traditional ascetic devotion with activist social service. By his death in 1830, the group had almost two million members. The new organization is one of the first of the major modern Hindu organizations. Ramanand Swami provided the transition from the standard eighteenth-century decentralized forms of religious piety to the more clearly structured, modern style of Hindu associations that emerged in the nineteenth century. While no individual association became a dominant expression of modern Hinduism, the more bureaucratic and centralized organizational format pioneered by Ramanand Swami and Swaminarayan did become the major way that modern-style Hindu associations operated.

In the final years of the eighteenth century, as in the opening years, many people believed that they were living in a time of great, possibly apocalyptic change. Joseph Priestley, an English Unitarian minister and pioneer of modern science affirmed in 1794, "If we can learn anything concerning what is before us, from the language of prophecy, great calamities . . . will precede that happy state of things, in which 'the kingdoms of this world' will become the 'kingdom of our Lord Jesus Christ.' . . . [T]he present disturbances in Europe [including the wars among the major powers following the French Revolution] are the beginning of those very calamitous times."[7] This sense that the end of the eighteenth century was a time of momentous change was shared by many around the world. Many of the followers of the Islamic teacher Osman Dan Fodio, who led a revivalist movement and jihad in West Africa at the turn of the century, believed him to be the Mahdi, the expected leader who would establish justice and true faith on earth before the end of time. In China, the followers of the White Lotus movement in their revolt in the 1790s believed in the imminent appearance of Buddha Maitreya, ushering in a new age. In Europe, people cited the prophecy of Nostradamus that in the year 1792 there would be persecutions and "a renovation of the age."[8] Many joined Priestley in interpreting the dramatic events of the French Revolution in apocalyptic terms of prophecies being fulfilled.

World historical transformations *were* taking place at the end of the eighteenth century, but they were not the expected apocalyptic ones. The emergence of new modes of human community at the beginning of the modern age was a change that is possibly as profound as the Agricultural Revolution or the development of cities as the core of large scale societies. The old lifestyles, however, did not suddenly disappear; the older dynamics of interactions of ways of life persisted. The long term decline of the hunting-gathering way of life continued as agriculturalists and urban-based agents expanded control in the remaining areas in which hunting-gathering peoples survived. A few, like the Inuit in the Arctic regions of North America or groups in the vast Amazon rain forests, maintained the old lifestyles, protected by their isolation. Although the Sami peoples in Scandinavia were under pressure to change their ways of living, a reference work on universal history published in 1795 could still report that the "Laplanders," or the Sami people, could be "said to be under no regular government" and in their lands there are "no gardens planted by the hand of man."[9]

However, most hunter-gatherers shared the continuing experiences of the San in Southwest Africa or the Chukchi in northeast Siberia. Some San became farmers like the Bantu and Dutch groups that were expanding into their lands, while the South African governments forcibly resettled others as poor laborers, and many were killed. The Chukchi way of life was based on reindeer husbandry and was a self-sufficient subsistence economy. Reindeer provided milk and meat in their diets, materials for their clothing, and mobility with reindeer-drawn sleds. The Chukchi resisted Russian military advances during the eighteenth century, but their reindeer-based economy changed as they were increasingly integrated into the Siberian market economy. They became subjects in the Russian Empire by the early nineteenth century.

By the end of the eighteenth century, no nomadic society or chieftaincy was in a position to conquer any urban society. The last such conquest was the Manchu invasion of China in the seventeenth century. However, new products, like firearms, and new resources like horses, made it possible for some chieftaincies to become more powerful by creating new ways of controlling people and resources.

The Comanches of the Great Plains in North America provide a dramatic example of the transformation of non-urban agricultural society in the eighteenth century. Originally a marginal hunting-gathering people, they became a powerful network of warrior bands because of their innovative integration of horses into their culture. The Spanish introduced horses into the Western Hemisphere in the sixteenth century. By the seventeenth century both domestic and wild horses were numerous in the plains north of Mexico. Most of the local peoples made limited use of horses, but by the beginning of the eighteenth century, the Comanches were experts in horse management and emerged as a powerful nomadic society. During the century, they successfully defeated most of their Native American rivals, fought Spanish expansion into their territories, and became active participants in trade networks. In an 1805 report, an American general stated a consensus view that the Comanches "constitute the most powerful nation of savages on this continent."[10] The efficient mobility for the nomadic communities provided by the horses and the military tactics effectively using horses developed by the Comanches during the eighteenth century enabled them to remain a power until the defeat of their last major warrior-chief, Quanah Parker, in 1874.

In the island societies of the Pacific, long term trends of centralization of control over clusters of islands continued and were given strength by the new resources available in the eighteenth century. The Hawaiian Islands came under the control of a single major chieftain, Kamehameha, who came to power in 1782. The emerging power of Kamehameha was based on a combination of the long-term development of irrigation agriculture and the formation of a political system that transcended kin-based allegiances to local chiefs. The new kingdom was not itself a "modern" state but established the bridge between the eighteenth-century structures of major chieftaincies and the later nineteenth-century kingdom.

Similar centralization of control occurred in the Tahiti islands and in Tonga. In Tahiti, a strong chieftain united the many separate chieftaincies described by Lewis de Bougainville in 1768 into a single kingdom. This new ruler brought an end to the previous balance of power among rival leaders, creating the foundation for a centralized monarchy. He adopted the name of Pomare and ruled as king or regent from 1789 to 1803. His son, Pomare II (r. 1803–21), worked with the Christian missionaries who came to Tahiti during his reign to consolidate the power of the dynasty. A missionary who worked with him said that Pomare II wanted "to become the universal monarch of the Islands of

This petroglyph in a Wyoming canyon represents a horse and a Comanche rider in the time of the expansion of Comanche power in the Central Plains of North America. The horses brought by the Spaniards enabled the Comanches change from hunting-gathering peoples into a warrior nation. Richard Collier, Photographer, Wyoming State Historic Preservation Office, Department of State Parks and Cultural Resources

the Pacific Ocean and through the profession of [Christian] faith in the King of kings to make himself a King of kings."[11] A little later, Taufa'ahau (George Tupou I) transformed the old maritime network of trade centered in Tonga into a dynastic monarchy that survived into the twenty-first century.

Another major world historical transformation that was dramatic but not apocalyptic was the changing nature of urban life. The "great cities" prior to the eighteenth century were primarily capital cities and centers of empires. After 1700, the expanding networks of trade and the

A CANOE of the SANDWICH ISLANDS, the ROWERS MASKED.

The canoes of Pacific island peoples, like this Hawaiian (Sandwich Island) vessel, made travel across great distances possible. They were an important resource for the military expansion by local island rulers who were creating major chieftaincies in the eighteenth century. John Webber c. 1785, David Rumsey Historical Map Collection

mass markets for new products provided the foundations on which great commercial centers were built. One of the first of the new commercial centers was Amsterdam, the home base for the Dutch East India Company established in 1602. Although Amsterdam was the center of a small country, during the seventeenth and eighteenth centuries it became a powerful economic center in Europe. It was described in a compilation of travelers' accounts as "a place of no great antiquity" but having "a very large share of the commerce carried on in the four quarters of the globe."[12] Its bankers and financial institutions developed efficient services for international trade, and many of the products bound for Western Europe passed through its port.

In Mughal India, the "company towns" in which the East India Company was based outpaced the older imperial centers. Bombay (now Mumbai), Madras (now Chennai), and Calcutta (now Kolkata) were transformed from marginal urban areas into major centers of Indian urban economy. Similarly, changes in Qing commercial policies in China opened the way for Shanghai to become a major commercial hub. In 1730, an imperial edict moved the main office of "river and sea customs" for the region to Shanghai. The provincial governor noted that "Shanghai is a remote place where there are many coves by the sea where evildoers can appear and disappear at will . . . [but with] the appointment of a circuit intendant to make inspections. . . . Shanghai will be transformed into a safe place."[13] Although Shanghai was not intensively involved in trade with Europeans, it became a commercial center in the domestic cotton, tea, and grain markets and much of the growing trade with Japan passed through the city. These activities laid the foundations for Shanghai to become one of the major centers of China's global trade. Shanghai emerged as one of the new type of cities, like Amsterdam, that were important centers of trade and commerce different from the older type of cities as centers of imperial power and administration.

These new commercial urban centers were not "modern" industrial cities. They were products of the networks of economic and political interactions that had shaped global relations since the sixteenth century. The basic sources of their wealth were still agricultural productivity and the work urban artisans, and not yet the productivity of industrial factories.

However, these eighteenth-century commercial cities presage one of the major features of industrial society. The majority of the population in the major societies around the world was still rural but the commercial cities were part of the increasing urbanization of the population. These new cities also indicate the increase in power of new groups. In a city like Amsterdam, merchants, artisans, and financiers, rather than aristocracy and clergy, dominated civic life and politics. Wharves and markets were more important than palaces and cathedrals.

Revolutions and reform programs reshaped political systems around the globe at the same time that trade and financial networks created new patterns of urban life. Great transformations were taking place but they were not the theological apocalyptic changes expected by many. Some, like Tobias Lear, reporting on conditions in Haiti during the revolution to the United States secretary of state, James Madison, believed that "A new and important Symbol Aera [era] has commenced here" with the abolition of slavery and the proclamation that "All men, regardless of color, are eligible to all employment."[14] Lear was describing a critical step in the end of the eighteenth-century plantation system in general, not just a local development. In terms of political revolution, he described the first independent non-European-based state to be created by the rejection of the European imperial systems of overseas colonies.

The Haitian Revolution was in the middle of the era spanning the end of the eighteenth and the beginning of the nineteenth centuries that is frequently identified as the Age of Revolution. The centerpieces of this age in many people's minds are the American (1775–83) and French (1789–99) Revolutions. Although these revolutions provide important foundations for future modern political systems and are often central in narratives of modernity, they are historically embedded in eighteenth-century realities. In the contexts of the actual developments at the time, these movements began as revolts against eighteenth-century political systems.

The thirteen Anglophone British colonies on the Atlantic coast of North America had a variety of flexible relationships with the government in London. However, the expenses of the global campaigns of the Seven Years' War (1756–63) and the intensification of world trade networks changed these relationships by the final third of the eighteenth century. The central government intensified its regulation of colonial economic (and political) activities in the 1760s and early 1770s, reflecting similar efforts by officials in London to gain more control over activities of the East India Company (EIC) in South Asia. The Regulating Act of 1773, which was a major step in the takeover of EIC by the central government in London, came in the same year as the Boston Tea Party, a protest against central government taxation policies in the colonies. Both colonial taxation and EIC control were part of the consolidation of royal influence in the British parliament under the leadership of Frederick North, whose family had global economic and political interests, in the 1770s. These policies reflect the broader eighteenth-century trend of governmental centralization on a global scale.

The Boston Tea Party protests were soon followed by the establishment of a Continental Congress and armed clashes between protest militias and British troops in 1775. The American Revolution formally began with the Declaration of Independence in 1776. This Declaration reflects the themes of many late eighteenth-century revolutions. The main body of the Declaration is a protest against centralized states, whose policies are viewed as "a long train of abuses and usurpations," drawing the conclusion that a "prince whose character is thus marked by every act which may define a tyrant is unfit to be the ruler of a free people." Even among the revolutionaries who opposed monarchy as an institution, notably Thomas Paine in *Common Sense*, their positions tended to be more in line with eighteenth-century Enlightenment rationalist ideas about liberty and republicanism than the nineteenth-century modern visions of populist and national democracy. Paine's pamphlet is primarily an argument for independence from the British monarchy, concluding that "independence is the only bond that can tie and keep us together," and his closing sentence describes an Enlightenment commonwealth more than a modern nation-state: "Let the names of Whig and Tory [the major parties in the British parliament] be extinct; and let none other be heard among us, than those of a good citizen, an open and resolute friend, and a virtuous supporter of the rights of mankind and of the free and independent states of America."[15] This Enlightenment ideal commonwealth was proclaimed in the Constitution of the Commonwealth of Massachusetts in 1780 as a non-partisan body politic in which "the whole people covenants with each citizen, and each citizen with the whole people" for "the common good."[16]

Some foundations for populist governance are in the Declaration. The most frequently-quoted words in later years foreshadow a modern-style democratic state: "We hold these truths to be self-evident, that all men are created equal"; and governments derive "their just powers from the consent of the governed." However, it was the federal Constitution, adopted by the thirteen states in 1789, that institutionalized these principles in an elected presidency. This political system was confirmed by the peaceful transfer of power in 1800 from one president who lost an election to a newly elected president. Thomas Jefferson, the author of the basic draft of the Declaration as well as the victorious presidential candidate in the 1800 election, spoke of a double revolution, with the "revolution of 1800" being "as real a revolution in the principles of our government as that of 1776 was in its form; not effected indeed by the sword, as that, but by the rational and peaceful instrument of reform, the suffrage of the people."[17] Jefferson's two revolutions were the two dimensions of revolution in this era: a protest against eighteenth-century governance and the foundations for a modern representative political system.

In the French Revolution, the transition from an eighteenth-century revolution to a revolution demanding modern populist governance was rapid. The beginning of the revolution was a period of revolt against abuses of the eighteenth-century system, with the aim of correction. Early protests in 1787 arose when the government faced a financial crisis and proposed a major new tax to a specially convened Assembly of Notables, a body of nobles and clergy that had not met for more than a century. When the Assembly rejected the plan and asked for a permanent representative body, the king and his ministers tried to gain approval from other bodies to force approval. When the king,

Patriotic engravings like this portrait of President John Adams were popular in the time before the strongly contested election of 1800 in the United States. Thomas Jefferson defeated the incumbent Adams in that election, confirming the democratic nature of the new American Constitutional system. Library of Congress Prints and Photographs Division

Louis XVI, was told by his cousin, the duke of Orléans, that his action was illegal, the king responded: "I want it, so it is legal."[18] This petulant response reflected monarchical absolutism that was out of touch with political realities.

SERMENT DU JEU DE PAUME, A VERSAILLES.
le 20 Juin 1789.

Deputies of the Third Estate (commoners as opposed to aristocrats and clergy) met in a tennis court in Versailles in 1789 when they were excluded from the meeting of the Estates General. They swore an oath of commitment to reform (the Tennis Court Oath) in a major early action in the French Revolution. Library of Congress Prints and Photographs Division

Louis XVI was forced to call the first meeting since 1614 of the Estates General, a legislative body that included the First Estate of the clergy, the Second Estate of the nobility, and the Third Estate, which included everyone else. The most powerful groups in the Third Estate were urban professionals (lawyers, bankers, and business people) and others in the emerging middle class. Under the leadership of the Third Estate, the Estates General transformed itself into the National Assembly in 1789 and took an oath of solidarity. Its first decree affirmed that it had been called to, among other things, "maintain the true principles of monarchy."[19] The revolution was still a protest within the terms of eighteenth-century politics.

By 1792 to 1793, the new visions of radicals became the program of the second revolutionary style, laying the foundations for a populist and eventually nationalist political system. Efforts within the new Assembly to create a constitutional monarchy failed, and an elected National Convention proclaimed a republic in 1792. The revolutionaries adopted the guillotine as the means to execute enemies of the revolution, and the destruction of the French aristocracy began. Louis XVI was executed in 1793, confirming the establishment of a radical republican regime. Although the establishment of an autocratic imperial system by Napoleon in 1799 and, following his defeat in 1815, the restoration of the Bourbon dynasty, brought an end to populist republicanism for a time, revolutionary France provided inspiration and prototypes for nationally identified revolutions and populist movements throughout the modern era.

Around the globe, revolutionaries followed the path of the French and American revolutions. Some uprisings were directly associated with those two events, either by ideological inspiration or French conquest and overthrow of old systems. The Polish Revolution in 1794 was led by Thaddeus Kosciuszko, a soldier who had fought for the American Revolution, and looked to revolutionary France for support and inspiration. He organized opposition to the partitions of Polish lands by the great powers of Russia, Prussia, and Austria, and his short-lived regime recognized peasants as well as nobility as part of the Polish nation. Similar revolutionary movements developed throughout Europe, and Dutch, Swiss, and Italian revolutionary republics were established following victories by French armies over the old states.

Revolutions in this era were not confined to Europe, but often those in other continents had different objectives and consequences. Revolts in Vietnam, West Africa, Spanish America, and China were some of the many non-European revolutions that created new political structures and ideological visions, reflecting the increasing globalization of even local socio-political dynamics. Vietnam was formally ruled by the Lê dynasty, which had united the country in the fifteenth century. However, since the sixteenth century, the country had been controlled by two great families, the Trinh in the north and the Nguyên in the south. During the eighteenth century, increasing commercial activities and growth of domestic and international trade changed social status structures, and European traders and missionaries were more actively involved in local political and economic affairs.

Factors like these produced growing discontent among peasants and urban workers. This unrest created support for the revolt beginning in 1771 led by three brothers from the area of Tây Son, who adopted the family name of Nguyên. A later report in 1799 by an official of the old Nguyên family described them as common people with a large following: "The brothers Nhac and Huê were people of cotton cloth, who did not have an inch of land to poke a stick into. Despite this, they raised their arms and voices as one, and people followed them by the tens of thousands."[20] The Tây Son movement defeated both of the old dominant families and took control of the Lê dynasty's court. When a large Chinese army invaded the country in 1788 in support of the Lê emperor, the leading general in the revolt declared himself emperor with the reign name of Quang Trung and defeated the Chinese. The new state faced rivalries within the new ruling family and old regional divisions. The Nguyên family was able to revive its military force and in 1802 defeated the less effective leaders who succeeded Quang Trung. The resulting Nguyên dynastic state built on political foundations laid during the Tây Son era. They ruled throughout the nineteenth century, and survived at least nominally, under French control, until 1945.

A local Islamic teacher in what is modern Nigeria, Uthman Dan Fodio, organized a jihad against local rulers in 1804. He agreed with his teacher, al-Mukhtar al-Kunti, who said that his region "is a land where unbelief prevails among the majority of the people and all the Muslims there are under the domination of the unbelievers whom they have recognized as rulers."[21] Many local people followed his call to mobilize for Islamic renewal.

Dan Fodio's movement was part of a long tradition of revivalist religious movements in West Africa. The political systems that had developed by the eighteenth century in the sudanic regions were careful syntheses of indigenous traditions of sacred kingship and the teachings of Muslim mystical brotherhoods that were willing to accept local cultural practices and popular religious rituals as a part of Muslim life. Tensions built up between local rulers and reformist Islamic teachers who urged greater adherence to Islamic law and called for an end to practices associated with pre-Islamic traditions of popular magic. The disagreements at times led to active reformist movements and, in some cases, jihads which overthrew of the old regimes and then established political systems more explicitly identified as Islamic. Dan Fodio's jihad resulted not only in the overthrow of the local ruler but spread to other states in the region. The leading state of this cluster of jihad emirates was the caliphate of Sokoto, established in 1812 and led by Dan Fodio's son. These emirates became the basis for political organization in Muslim Nigeria during the nineteenth century and still exist as socio-political units within Nigeria in the twenty-first century.

In Spanish America, the Bourbon dynasty that was established in Spain as a result of the War of the Spanish Succession at the beginning of the century began a program of reforms to bring the colonies more closely under the control of the central monarchy. These policies heightened existing tensions between the creoles (descendants of early colonizers) and more recently arrived officials from Spain. These conflicts led, in part, to the wars for independence at the beginning of the nineteenth century. However, the largest actual revolts in the late eighteenth century involved uprisings by indigenous peoples hoping to re-establish the pre-Spanish social order.

In 1780, José Gabriel Túpac Amaru, a Native American leader, began a major indigenous rebellion against the colonial system. His movement had some appeal to *mestizos* and creoles. A popular priest identified him as an "instrument of the Lord . . . for the correction of many wrongs."[22] However, his primary appeal came from his claim to leadership as a descendant of the pre-colonial Inca rulers. His support utilized a synthesis similar to the earlier Antonian movement in the Kongo, combining indigenous religious traditions with the Catholicism of incoming Europeans. The Bishop of Cozco described this position, saying that the indigenous people "convince us that they adore the true God only when they see Him dressed like the Incas, whom they believed to be deities."[23] The revolt was forcefully crushed by the armies of the Spanish colonial administration in 1783. It illustrates the important type of revolution of the late eighteenth century that is both a product of eighteenth-century developments like the centralizing reforms of the Spanish Bourbons and an attempt to reject those developments in a movement to restore the old Inca society.

Revolutionary movements in China rose against the centralization of the Qing dynasty. Opposition to government corruption and repression in China often took the form of religious movements within the framework of populist Buddhist sects. The White Lotus sectarian tradition, with roots in the twelfth century, provided inspiration for a number of opposition groups in the late eighteenth century. In 1796 disputes between some local government offices and members of one of these groups in the White Lotus tradition, possibly involving taxes or extortions by the officials, led to a rebellion that gained support from White Lotus sectarian groups in five provinces. Sectarian military forces, especially under the command of Wang Cong'er, a woman whose husband had been executed for sectarian activities, were successful against imperial armies for almost a decade. The rebellion was finally crushed in 1804, but its popularity and successes weakened the Qing state and laid foundations for populist revolts during the nineteenth century. Although the Qing Empire was weakened by the White Lotus and other rebellions, it survived as one of the most powerful empires in the world.

The imperial monarchies all faced revolutionary threats. In 1773–76, the Pugachev rebellion was possibly the largest peasant revolt in Russian history, and the Napoleonic wars were threats to Romanov rule. However, under the leadership of Alexander I (r. 1801–25), Russia was one of the major European powers. Although the Habsburgs terminated the title of Holy Roman Emperor in 1806, the reformulated Austrian Empire survived a variety of nationalist movements. The German states were humiliatingly defeated by Napoleon's armies and the result was a surge in German national feeling. In Prussia it was King Frederick William III (r. 1797–1840) who issued the call "To My People" (*An mein Volk*) to rise up in the War of Liberation against Napoleon in 1813 and whose government set in motion major reforms, creating the modern Prussian state. In France, the Constitutional Charter of 1814 in restoring the Bourbon monarchy affirmed that "all authority in France resides in the person of the king."

Most of the major monarchical states around the world survived the challenges of the age of revolutions. In Europe, the survival was most clearly presented in the continental negotiations at the Congress of Vienna in 1814–15, which defined the end of the French Revolutionary and Napoleonic period. However, even Napoleon's vision was not one of populist nationalism or republicanism, or a Europe consisting of modern sovereign nation-states. Instead, his vision, as described by Count Klemens von Metternich in 1809 while he was the Austrian representative to Napoleon, fits more into the pattern of the Holy Roman Empire, which had just been eliminated by the Napoleonic wars: "The division of Europe into Powers, of which the strongest would not have been more than three or four millions of subjects, has for some time been in Napoleon's plan. . . . To create a vast empire, to become chief and protector of twenty or thirty small states, such was the design at which Napoleon aimed."[24]

The Congress and other negotiations created what has been called the "Vienna System," which confirmed dynastic state legitimacy and sovereignty within clearly defined borders. This system preserved the multi-ethnic states under dynastic rule, as they had developed in the eighteenth century. These experiences show the survival ability of the dynastic state systems. In confronting the revolutions and rebellions of the era, the monarchies were able to undertake significant reforms.

It was a time of revolutions and political survivals as states and societies around the globe began their diverse transitions to modernity.

Ramanand Swami, the devotional teacher in Gujarat in India, was part of major religious transitions similar to the political changes. In the account presented by this movement of its history, Ramanand Swami proclaimed himself "as a mere drum beater, heralding the arrival of the chief player." In describing this predicted figure, Ramanand said, "Just as Krishna is greater than all other incarnations, He is even greater than Krishna."[25] In this way, as one study describes this for Western readers, Ramanand "appears in the story in the role of a John the Baptist who prepares the way for a greater teacher," with that teacher, Swaminarayan, becoming "the last of the medieval saints and the first of the modern sadhus of neo-Hinduism."[26]

The abolitionist movement was also, to a remarkable degree, an early modern-style protest movement. Its goal was the abolition of slavery, especially plantation slavery as it had developed in the West Indies. The basic lines of debate were not expressed so much in modern terms of human rights as in the terms of eighteenth-century evangelical social conscience. John Wesley was one of the early significant advocates of abolition and his "Thoughts Upon Slavery," written in the 1770s, set the common tone in admonishing the British plantation owners: "The just GOD will reward every man according to his works. . . . Then will the great GOD deal with *you*, as you have dealt with *them* [slaves], and require all their blood at your hands. . . . Regard not money! All that a man hath will he give for his life? Whatever you lose, lose not your soul: nothing can countervail that loss. Immediately quit the horrid trade: At all events, be an honest man."[27]

The center of the abolitionist movement was William Wilberforce, an influential politician and philanthropist person who came from a wealthy British business family with global trade connections, especially in the Russian trade. Some important members of his extended family were deeply involved in the pietist-evangelical revival, and important activists joining Wilberforce in the abolitionist movement included leaders in the nascent Industrial Revolution, like Josiah Wedgwood. Wilberforce, after he announced his adherence to evangelical Christianity, declared in his diary in 1787, "God almighty has set before me two great objects: the suppression of the slave trade and the reformation of manners," by which he meant a transformation of social morality.[28] He undertook both of these tasks within the framework of an evangelical religious reformism, in which he argued that the "professed Christians of the higher and middle classes" had little knowledge of "real Christianity."

Cartoons were an important weapon in the abolitionist battle against the institutions of slavery. Depictions of the cruelty of the slave traders as in this cartoon helped the general public to become aware of the viciousness of the trade. Library of Congress Prints and Photographs Division

Their "opinions on the subject of religion are not formed from the perusal of the word of God. The Bible lies on the shelf unopened: and they would be wholly ignorant of its contents," and the solution is the "diligent perusal of the Holy Scriptures."[29] His view of slavery was similar to Wesley's in being seen through the perspective of eighteenth-century pietism. In closing his address to Parliament in 1791, he, like Wesley, identified participation in the slave trade as a matter of guilt before God: "Never never will we desist till we have wiped away this scandal from the Christian name [and] released ourselves from the load of guilt under which we at present labour."[30]

Although Wilberforce's abolitionist movement was rooted in eighteenth-century evangelical pietism, it also developed methods of popular protest characteristic of modern political activism.[31] The passage of a bill by the British parliament in 1807 abolishing the slave trade in British areas marked a major step in the ending of the eighteenth-century plantation system around the world.

Significant religious movements in other major traditions were similar links between eighteenth-century institutions and modern ones. In Japan, some scholars revived the indigenous traditions of Shinto faith and ritual in the late eighteenth century. The emperor had occupied the center of the political system since early medieval times. Japanese imperial society was strongly influenced by Confucian and Buddhist ideas coming from China. During the sixteenth century, following a period of decentralization, powerful military war lords unified the country. At the same time, Japan came into significant contact with Europeans, who converted a small number of Japanese to Christianity. In the seventeenth century, the Tokugawa shoguns (military commanders) consolidated their power and adopted a conscious policy of isolation from the rest of the world. During the eighteenth century, within the framework of the shogunate and self-conscious isolation, some religious thinkers and intellectuals developed distinctive interpretations of the Shinto tradition, with a new emphasis on reverence for the emperor and on affirmation of Japanese traditions.

By the late eighteenth century, these developments resulted in the growing influence of the school of "national learning" (*Kokugaku*), a group of Shinto thinkers who worked to identify the true Japanese identity by studying the early traditions of Japanese imperial culture and making the public more aware of their original content. In the eighth century, the stories of the beginnings of Japanese society had been compiled in a "Record of Ancient Matters" (*Kojiki*) and a millennium later a series of reformist scholars worked to redefine the imperial ideology in indigenous Shinto terms through a detailed study of the early texts. This effort involved a rejection of Chinese influences, as one of the leaders in the movement, Motoori Norinaga, made clear: "In ancient times, although there was no prosy system of doctrine in Japan there were no popular disturbances, and the empire was peacefully ruled. It is because the Japanese were truly moral in their practice that they required no theory of morals, and the fuss made by the Chinese about theoretical morals is owing to their laxity in practice."[32] Motoori affirmed the unique superiority of the Japanese worldview: "The eternal endurance of the dynasty of the Mikados is a complete proof that the 'way' called *Kami no michi* or Shintō infinitely surpasses the systems of all other countries."[33]

The "National Learning" movement aimed at the restoration of real sovereignty to the emperor and the affirmation of a distinctive Japanese identity framed in terms of the Shinto tradition. In many ways, it laid the intellectual and cultural foundations for the actual restoration of the emperor in 1868, a moment considered to be the beginning of modern Japanese history. In the Muslim world similar movements of transition developed. In India, Shah Abd al-Aziz, the son of the eighteenth-century advocate of Islamic renewal, Shah Wali Allah, succeeded his father (who died in 1763) as an important teacher of *hadith* (Traditions of the Prophet) and the Qur'an in Delhi. However, the growing control by the British changed the context within which the call for renewal of faith was articulated. For most practical purposes, Muslim rule was finished. Shah Abd al-Aziz formally recognized this in a fatwa (formal presentation of an Islamic legal position) in 1803, in which he declared, "Promulgation of the command of *kufr* [unbelief] means that in the matter of administration and the control of the people . . . the *kāfir*s act according to their discretion. . . . From here [Delhi] to Calcutta the Christians are in complete control."[34]

Shah Abd al-Aziz's recognition of new realities set in motion two movements that shaped modern Muslim life in South Asia. The first was a continuation of scholarly reform in which the ulama continued to provide guidance for Muslims in civil relations and religious affairs. The network of scholars in the intellectual and religious tradition of Shah Wali Allah utilized the newly available resources of printing presses as well as lectures and public debates. Shah Abd al-Aziz issued numerous fatwas, and he and his associates provided intellectual foundations for reform movements that emerged later in the century. The second movement was the call for jihad against unbelievers. Although Shah Abd al-Aziz's 1803 fatwa is frequently cited as opening the way for jihad against British rule, when his disciple Ahmad Barelwi declared a jihad against unbelievers, it was against rulers who were Sikhs, a growing religious tradition in northwest India. The jihad combined opposition to non-Muslim rule over Muslims with rejection of adoption of non-Muslim devotional practices, which, in the words of Shah Wali Allah's grandson, Shah Ismail, let "evil ideas mingle in the stream of a religion."[35] Although the jihad was quickly defeated, Barelwi's movement inspired other Muslim militants, like Titu Mian in Bengal, and later Pan-Islamic groups as a model of a revivalist movement. In these two different ways, Shah Abd al-Aziz was an important bridge between eighteenth-century and modern societies in South Asia.

The revolutionary movements of the late eighteenth century also had significant religious dimensions. The two prototypical Western revolutions—the American and the French—produced reactions even in major conservative religious institutions. The papacy faced major challenges as a result of the French Revolution and the subsequent conquests of papal domains in Italy by Napoleon. In that context, the Bishop of Imola, who would later become Pope Pius VII, reflected the new positive meaning of "democracy" in his 1797 Christmas Eve sermon: "The form of democratic government adopted among us, most beloved brethren . . . is not inconsistent with the Gospel. . . . The Catholic religion is the thing most precious to your hearts. . . . Do not believe that it is opposed to the form of democratic government. . . . Be good Christians, beloved brethren, and you will be the best democrats."[36] In 1801, he signed the concordat with Napoleon, which was a crucial part of the modern redefinition of church-state relations. He also presided over the church's conservative role in the political restorations in Europe after the fall of Napoleon.

At the same time, Catholic leaders in the newly independent United States petitioned the Vatican to be freed from the jurisdiction of the Vicar Apostolick of London. John Carroll, the priest who wrote the request and ultimately became the first Catholic bishop in the United States in 1789, had been active in the revolution and his cousin, Charles Carroll, was a signer of the Declaration of Independence. In his letter, John Carroll affirmed the religious significance as well as the political importance of the American Revolution: "You are not ignorant, that in these United States our Religious system has undergone a revolution, if possible, more extraordinary, than our political one. In all of them, free toleration is allowed to Christians of every denomination. . . . This is a blessing and advantage, which is our duty to preserve and improve with the utmost prudence."[37] The religious and democratic revolutions in America described by Carroll and Jefferson became integral parts of the modern ideals of state and society.

Religion was also an important element in the development of modern scientific thought and practice. The career of Joseph Priestley provides an example of the complexities of the changing cosmologies and worldviews in the latter part of the eighteenth century. Like Newton earlier and many other scientific thinkers of the time, Priestley wrote major works on religion and philosophy in addition to his volumes of scientific studies. In this, he viewed scientific study as a religious act: "The best founded praise is that which is due to the man, who, from a supreme veneration for the God of nature, takes pleasure in contemplating his *works*."[38] He presents in his writings, in his sermons, and in his reports on experiments a sense of a close relationship between his theology and his science. With this perspective, his life and work is a reminder of the continuing strength of religious worldviews, even in the contexts of the intellectual worlds of the Enlightenment and the Scientific Revolution.[39]

Priestley is considered one of the major figures in the development of modern chemistry. Along with Antoine Lavoisier, Priestley identified oxygen as a distinct gas, a landmark scientific discovery of the era. For more than a century, thinkers in Western Europe worked on redefining the longstanding understanding of the basic elements of the Aristotelean system: fire, air, water, and earth. In the seventeenth century, scholars developed a new approach involving a postulated substance called phlogiston, which was thought to be a fire-like element in combustible materials. Priestley became an advocate of the phlogiston theory and, in the course of his experiments, he isolated oxygen, although he understood it in terms of the theory as "dephlogisticated air." Lavoisier was an opponent of the theory and in his studies of gases, he developed a terminology in which he gave the name "oxygen" to this component of air. Lavoisier was ultimately able to disprove the phlogiston theory, providing a foundation for modern chemistry.

The debate about phlogiston exemplifies the character of emerging scientific thought in the eighteenth century. Intellectuals in the emerging "sciences" engaged in debates in which they developed new modes of analysis. These disputes were not fights between upholders of a classical or medieval cosmology and advocates of a new-style science, as was the case in the experiences of Copernicus or Galileo. The phlogiston theory was developed in the seventeenth century as an alternative to the established cosmology, and the debates about this theory were within the conceptual framework of eighteenth-century scientific thought. Neither Priestley nor Lavoisier was medieval in his methods or conclusions, but they both also were still operating as natural philosophers, not scientists. Priestley spoke of his research as being in "experimental philosophy" in which "by pursuing even false lights, real and important truths may be discovered."[40]

These intellectuals defined the foundations for the emerging disciplines of the modern sciences. Lavoisier not only helped to define modern chemistry through his experiments, but also, in a collaborative project he developed a systematic nomenclature that is still central to the modern study of chemistry.[41] He proclaimed that the study of air and gases was "destined to bring about a revolution in physics and in chemistry."[42] The emerging revolutionary worldviews in science were not isolated from the politics of the time. Priestley was a strong supporter of the French Revolution, and as an English Unitarian minister he joined others in viewing the events of the late eighteenth century in apocalyptic terms. He viewed the French Revolution as a sign of the imminent Second Coming of Christ. Demonstrations and physical threats in

England forced him to move to the new United States. In contrast, Lavoisier, as an official in the Old Regime in France, was guillotined during the Reign of Terror in 1794.

Economic developments matched the dramatic political and scientific changes of the era. The economic transformations fall under the general label of the Industrial Revolution. Ellen Hacking's small device for carding cotton was a part of this broad process. Arnold Toynbee, a nineteenth-century British economic historian and uncle of the world historian of the same name, popularized this label for the transformations in an influential series of lectures. In his words, this revolution "destroyed the old world and built a new one. . . . Villages became towns, towns became cities, and factories started up on barren heath and deserted waste."[43] However, as dramatic as these changes were in shaping nineteenth-century societies around the globe and in creating the economic bases for modernity, this Industrial Revolution was just beginning at the end of the eighteenth century. Major developments from the middle of the eighteenth century continued to shape regional and global economic life, as well as providing frameworks for the emergence of modern-style industrial enterprise. Three trends from the mid-century—changing patterns of mass consumption, the development of plantation enterprises, and the evolution of large-scale monopoly trading companies—reflect these dynamics.

Growing consumer demand for products like coffee, cotton, tea, sugar, chocolate, and tobacco continued to shape global trade and production patterns. The demand for coffee, for example, continued to shape social and economic institutions from Java and Sumatra to Brazil, and sparked international interest in the revolution in Haiti.

In the global market for cotton cloth at the beginning of the century, India was the major producer and exporter. Key figures in this trade were merchant-traders like Mulla Abdul Ghafur of Surat. Cotton cloth became very popular in Western Europe. The sales of a very popular print design with a tear drop shape show how the textile trade changed. Shawls made in Kashmir utilized the design and it was used in cotton prints as well. At the end of the eighteenth century, the Scottish textile manufacturing town of Paisley began to mass produce cloth with this design, replacing imports from India. The popular design came to be identified, in the English-speaking world, with the name of this Scottish town. Another major market for cotton cloth was as a medium of exchange in the slave trade in Africa. Gradually, British entrepreneurs began to develop their capacity for producing larger quantities of cloth as a result a series of inventions (Hacking's carding device and more dramatically, industrial machinery like James Hargreaves's spinning jenny, which mechanized the process of spinning yarn) and the development, credited to Richard Arkwright, of coordinated production facilities or cotton mills. Many historians see these developments in Britain as the foundation for the whole Industrial Revolution and, more specifically, the basis of the modern factory system. Although the British cotton industry would come to dominate the world market in the nineteenth century, during the eighteenth it was simply emerging. In the 1770s when Arkwright and other investors created the pioneering mills at Cromford and elsewhere in Britain, British cotton goods remained unable to compete effectively with the less expensive cloth from India in the African market. Even in Britain, cotton cloth from India still set the standards. The new *Encyclopædia Britannica* in 1771 in its article on cotton stated, "The finest sort comes from Bengal and the coast of Coromandel."[44] The process of overtaking the Indians was relatively slow and was not completed until well into the nineteenth century.

In the global porcelain trade, the products of the great production facilities like Tang Ying's in Zingdezhen continued to dominate the market throughout the century. The success of Josiah Wedgwood in applying more factory-style methods in the production of high-quality earthenware laid the foundations for a modern industry in Britain. Wedgwood's creamware, especially his Queen's Ware, gained popularity and some success in the export market. He boasted, "Don't you think we shall have some Chinese Missionaries come here soon to learn the art of making Creamclour?"[45] However, although earthenware was popular, porcelain from Western Europe only gradually became a major commodity in the world markets.

A second major development continuing from mid-century is the evolution of slave-based plantations for the production of consumer products like sugar. By the end of the century, slavery had come under serious attack by the gradual successes of the abolitionist movement and the visibility of the revolution in Haiti. Although large-scale production of agricultural products still required inexpensive labor, a shift from slave labor to various forms of semi-coerced labor like indentured servitude or the use of cheap contract workers from South Asia developed as the plantation economies evolved. By the beginning of the nineteenth century, the slave-based plantation system was in decline.

The third element that was changing significantly was the organization of interregional trade. The great trade companies of the eighteenth century were gradually being replaced by direct forms of imperialism and new forms of corporate organization. During the Napoleonic wars at the end of the century, the British occupied the Southeast Asian territories of the Dutch East India Company. In the final treaty arrangements at the beginning of the nineteenth century, the Dutch regained control of the territories but as part of a Dutch overseas empire and the company ceased to exist. At the same time, the British company became a controlled subsidiary of the central government in London. New government bureaucracies replaced the companies as the European colonial empires of the nineteenth century emerged.

The new companies of importance in world trade were manufacturing firms producing textiles and other merchandise and they were not directly involved in managing the global trading networks. Financing for these new industrial enterprises was provided by new types of financial institutions, like joint-stock investment banks, which gradually replaced the entrepreneurial adventurers and family-based commercial banks as major sources of support.

The world in 1800 was very different from what it was in 1700. There were many political revolutions in a revolutionary age in which political systems were being transformed; there was a Scientific Revolution that was transforming the way humans understand the universe; there was an Industrial Revolution that was transforming economic life. However, the revolutions in political systems, in economics and industry, and in worldviews were not yet complete. It is in this dynamic mode that the eighteenth century chronologically came to an end.

Epilogue
The World in the Eighteenth Century

The Qianlong emperor of China sent a letter to King George III of England, in 1793, declaring, "We have never valued ingenious articles, nor do we have the slightest need of your country's manufactures."[1] This view contrasted with the views of his grandfather, the Kangxi emperor, at the beginning of the eighteenth century. The earlier emperor was reported by a European visitor to the Chinese court to have "received, very favourably, any foreigners skilled in such arts and sciences as were better understood in Europe than by his own subjects."[2] This visitor was part of the British mission to the Qianlong court led by George Macartney, a British nobleman with considerable experience in international business and colonial administration. Macartney's goal was to facilitate the expansion of trade by the British East India Company in China, and the emperor's letter to George III was in response to the Macartney mission.

The emperor's position was not an isolationist one. China had significant involvement in the world economy, achieving a very favorable balance of trade with the rest of the world through its exports of porcelains, silks, and tea. The emperor's assessment of Chinese needs for imports at that time was basically accurate. However, the global balance of power among the major societies was changing. The emperor's grandfather, Kangxi, could hold in detention an emissary from the pope, with no possibility of effective European retaliation, when the pope tried to discipline Jesuits in China. At the end of the eighteenth century, Macartney's evaluation of the power of the Chinese imperial state was that it "is an old, crazy, first rate man-of-war, which a fortunate succession of able and vigilant officers has contrived to keep afloat for these one hundred and fifty years past" but that it would drift and "be dashed to pieces on the shore."[3] Macartney's prediction was confirmed by the events of the nineteenth century.

Emperor Qianlong ruled China for more than sixty years in a time of expansion and economic development. He famously told a British emissary in 1793 that China had little need for European products and was in a position to enforce limitations of European involvement in Chinese affairs. © The Cleveland Museum of Art

Both Qianlong and Macartney were true products of eighteenth-century history. The emperor had been a patron of the great porcelain production facility run by Tang Ying and he led China in a time of economic growth and the expansion of China's sphere of power. Macartney was an important figure in the commercial and diplomatic relations of the day, serving as an envoy to the court of Catherine the Great, a governor in the West Indies, and a governor of Madras in the East India Company administration. He had great success as a leader in important eighteenth-century institutions. However, the encounter between the two men involved a sign of future relations as well as a continuation of the eighteenth-century economic balance in favor of the Chinese. Macartney arrived in a sixty-four-gun man-of-war that exhibited the future of military power in which the development of new technologies of weaponry would enable European, especially British, domination of the seas and land warfare. Neither the emperor nor Macartney would have envisioned the absolute upsetting of the balance of power in the crushing defeat of China in the Opium War of 1839–42, but the

British warship was a symbol of the coming change in global politics. The world of Qianlong was markedly different from that of Kangxi.

Two Quaker women in Pennsylvania also epitomize the changes of the century. At the beginning of the century, Mary Pennell told people to expect trying times and a great transformation. Her vision was framed in the apocalyptic expectations of the end of time. However, a century later, Elizabeth Griscom Ross Ashburn Claypoole, better known as Betsy Ross, participated in a very different transformation, the American Revolution. Betsy Claypoole was expelled from the Friends' (Quaker) fellowship and she joined the Free Quakers, an association of Quakers who had been similarly banished from their meetings because of their actions supporting the revolutionary cause. Their transgression, as the report of the Philadelphia meeting ejecting Samuel Wetherell stated, was that he "deviated from our ancient Testimony and peaceable principles, by manifesting himself a party in the public commotions prevailing, and taking a test of abjuration [of loyalty to the King] and allegiance [to the revolutionary movement]."[4] In later American patriotic narratives, Betsy Ross was identified as the woman who sewed the first flag of the new country. Although historians suggest that there were a number of people who made early flags, no one disputes her active support for the Revolution.

Mary Pennell participated in the creation of a new frontier community at the beginning of the eighteenth century. This self-identified commonwealth, Pennsylvania, was part of the growing globalization of economic, social, and political life in the distinctive conditions of the seventeenth and early eighteenth century. Betsy Ross also took part in the creation of a new community, but it was a nation created by one of the major revolutions of the late eighteenth century, not a religious commonwealth. This revolution provided the foundations for the building of a modern state in North America.

In India, new patterns of global trade as seen in the cotton trade reflected major changes in local and global economies. At the beginning of the century Mulla Abdul Ghafur of Surat controlled a network of workers who created some of the finest cotton cloth in the world, and he directed a fleet of ships that was an important part of the global cotton trade. In this trade, India was the dominant exporter of cotton in the world and Mulla Abdul Ghafur was a dominant leader in that economic system. However, as the British East India Company gained more power and influence both in India and in London, Surat lost its primary role in the cotton trade. The focus of political, military, and economic life shifted to the company center in Bombay. Mulla Abdul Ghafur's great-grandson, Mulla Fakruddin, moved to Bombay for a while. By the time he returned to Surat, the East India Company was successfully replacing Indian middlemen by "agents," paid employees of the company who dealt directly with the village weavers. In the words of various communications at the time from the Board of Trade in London, this reorganization would "recover to the Company that genuine knowledge of the business" that would facilitate getting more cloth at lower cost by freeing the company from what the Board of Trade called "Native Merchants of little property or probity."[5] Entrepreneurs like his grandfather were no longer central to the global trade in cotton. The merchants of the coastal trading system with their networks of weaving villages were being replaced by salaried employees and private British merchants who owned their own ships. The Mughal admiral who controlled Surat was defeated by the East India Company which in the words of an official gazetteer of the time, "obtained . . . the [power of making the] appointment to the post of admiral . . . by which their [the Company's] authority in this place became supreme."[6] The result was the decline of the Indian merchant fleets and middleman merchants like Mulla Abdul Ghafur. English traders and investors overcame the constraints of the Indian system and, along with the East India Company, transformed the patterns of trade and commerce in the Indian Ocean region.

The decline of India's role in the world cotton market had two important dimensions. The change in fortunes of the descendants of Mulla Abdul Ghafur is tied to developments characteristic of the eighteenth century—the rise of the large, integrated trade company with governmental responsibilities and its own military forces. The system of Mulla Abdul Ghafur did not require an army or navy, nor did he have to become a government administrator. However, his successors among the middleman merchants failed to develop these resources and were replaced by the distinctively eighteenth-century company.

The changes in the ways that cotton was purchased and sold in the world market were important and transformed the lives of merchants like Mulla Abdul Ghafur. By the nineteenth century, his role and reputation as a major merchant were replaced by popular legends about his wealth, as entrepreneurs like him were replaced by company agents. One such local legend was reported in a major gazetteer from the later time: "According to one story, the Mulla was, on one occasion, unfairly forced to take a cargo of spoiled goods. For a time he left the goods alone, and, when next he went to look at them, found diamonds and rubies instead of bad butter and damaged dates."[7] He was not remembered as a dominating merchant.

The second development in the decline of India's place in the global cotton market was even more dramatic. The new ways of producing cotton cloth that were associated with the factory system designed by Richard Arkwright in Britain ultimately replaced the old system of networks of weavers and artisans.

The shifts from Kangxi to Qianlong, from Mary Pennell to Betsy Ross, and from Mulla Abdul Ghafur to Richard Arkwright provide important frameworks for viewing the world of the eighteenth century.

The water frame designed by Richard Arkwright spun cotton thread in Arkwright's Cromford Mill and was a part of the technological developments in the early days of the Industrial Revolution. With the new cotton mills, Britain displaced India as the world's major source of cotton cloth. SSPL/Science Museum/Art Resource, NY

The earlier individuals were participants in the distinctive eighteenth-century experiences that were changing and sometimes transforming political, economic and religious life around the world. Their end-of-century counterparts were clearly shaped by and were products of these transformations that are at the heart of the special characteristics of eighteenth-century life. In the intervening years, the special eighteenth-century features of politics, economics, and religion developed in different ways around the world.

In political terms, the most powerful states of the eighteenth century were dynastic monarchies. The reforms of rulers like the Ottoman sultan, Ahmad III, and Catherine the Great in Russia involved creating increasingly centralized structures of rule. While they recognized the value of the cultures of their subjects, even in the European monarchies that had some national identities, the states were basically multi-ethnic and increasingly bureaucratic (rather than aristocratic) in nature. This type of state is the characteristic form of major states during the century. Although the revolutions and revolts in the final years of the century compelled monarchies to engage in important reforms, the survival of the major multi-ethnic imperial states in the early nineteenth century showed the strength of the eighteenth-century constructs. The rise to prominence of the nation-state was only beginning.

Economic life was also being reshaped during the eighteenth century. The increase in global trade and the establishment of large trading companies gave strength to the development of distinctively eighteenth-century economic enterprises like plantation economies and the slave trade. Increased production of products such as coffee, sugar, and cotton changed social structures in important ways in such areas as Brazil, India, and Java as well as in Europe and North America. However, the major transformations involved in what later was called the Industrial Revolution were only beginning. The great production center for Chinese porcelain led by Tang Ying was not yet a modern factory, and the cotton mill developed by Richard Arkwright was just a starting point for what was to come in the nineteenth century.

New types of religious movements, like Mary Pennell's Quakers, also gained importance during the eighteenth century. Some movements, such as the Antonian movement of Dona Beatriz in Kongo, show how the increasing globalization of human life shaped even distinctive local religious movements. Throughout the eighteenth century some intellectuals and religious teachers challenged existing cosmological and theological syntheses that were part of the traditions of faith and philosophy. In previous centuries comprehensive conceptual frameworks had become the foundations for belief and practice in public and private life. Neo-Confucianism in China, the natural theology of St. Thomas Aquinas, the consolidation of the schools of law in Islam, and similar compilations in other cultures became targets for critics during the eighteenth century.

Many of the critiques were framed in the religious terms of reform movements that called for interpreting the early sources and not being tied to the later interpretations that became associated with religious and political establishments. They were heirs to earlier criticisms of such establishments, like the sixteenth-century condemnations of Roman Church practices by Martin Luther and Ahmad al-Sirhindi's disapproval of the Mughal Sultan Akbar's political and religious pluralism. Reforms of this type are called for in the teachings of Muslim scholars like Shah Wali Allah in India and Muhammad ibn Abd al-Wahhab in Arabia and in the School of Han Learning in China. Often these movements created distinctive organizations that were different from the older communal structures of churches and temples. Pietists in Europe combined the "back-to-basics" approach with new types of organizations. At the end of the century, one of the largest of such movements was that of Ramanand Swami in India, whose work laid the foundations for a modern-style religious association in the nineteenth century.

Some of the critiques, especially in the West, involved thinking about the natural universe in new ways. In the first years of the eighteenth century, the visions of the natural world that Isaac Newton and others presented opened new ways of understanding how the universe works. Newtonian natural philosophy became, by the end of the century, an important framework supporting the emergence of what came later to be called the Scientific Revolution. During the century, important foundations were being laid for the development of modern scientific disciplines and methods. Georges-Louis Leclerc, Comte de Buffon, was helping to define what would become the modern biological sciences while Antoine Lavosier and Joseph Priestley were creating the discipline of modern chemistry. However, these efforts were still considered part of natural philosophy, not separate sciences. Like Newton before him, Priestley was a theologian as well as a scientist. The natural philosophy of that time was a distinctive product of eighteenth-century experiences, and modern science was only in its beginnings.

In the last years of the century, people in many parts of the world sensed these great changes. From the millennial expectations of the White Lotus revolts in China and the emerging jihad movements in India to the more secular revolutionaries in Napoleonic Europe, there was a sense that a new era was dawning. Reactions to the emerging European revolutions illustrate the spectrum of how people responded to the revolutions of the time. A prominent British conservative intellectual, John Bowles, spoke of the beginning of a new century, in 1800, as a time for serious reflection, especially since, in his view, "Never was the world in so calamitous or so perilous a state as at this moment."[8] In contrast, William Linn, a clergyman who served in the Continental Army during the American Revolution and was the first chaplain of the United States House of Representatives, looked back at the revolutions of the eighteenth century very differently. In a funeral eulogy for George Washington, he stated, "In the eighteenth century have flourished a number of the most eminent philosophers, historians, orators, patriots, and statesmen; the close of it has been eventful and astonishing beyond all precedent. . . . Memorable era! The age of great men, the age of extraordinary revolutions, the age of Washington."[9]

The eighteenth century is a memorable era. It is a time of transition to modernity, a time when the impact of the first globalization is being felt around the world. All of humanity was being brought into the webs of economic, cultural, and political interactions. Old ways of life disappeared as new ways of organizing human life emerged.

The lives and careers of the Kangxi and Qianlong emperors, Mary Pennell and Betsy Ross, and Mulla Abdul Ghafur and Richard Arkwright demonstrate that many of the major developments in the eighteenth century were neither medieval nor modern. The Qing dynasty was different from the "classical" imperial systems, the apocalyptic worldview of Mary Pennell came out of the religious fervor of the seventeenth century more than medieval Christianity, and Mulla Abdul Ghafur was in many ways the product of the new more global markets for consumer goods like cotton cloth. However, at the end of the century, Qianlong was not yet facing modern-style military forces. The new United States was only beginning to be the modern democratic nation-state that it would become during the nineteenth century, and the Industrial Revolution was only beginning during the lifetime of Arkwright.

Acknowledgments

Over the years, many people have been of great help to me in studying world history. They have helped me in my teaching and research and collectively their influence helped to shape my study of a world history of the eighteenth century. I owe a special intellectual debt to William H. McNeill, who was developing new ways of looking at world history at the time that I was beginning to teach courses in world history, and I am especially grateful to Marshall G. S. Hodgson, who gave me important advice on organizing courses in world history as well as defining important conceptual approaches to the study of world history.

I am grateful for the help and encouragement that I have received over the years from colleagues and friends in the University of New Hampshire and Georgetown University, and students have provided important new insights and inspiration. Institutionally, the World History Association provides a supportive community of scholars.

I give special thanks for the patience and strong editorial guidance that Nancy Toff and her associates at Oxford University Press have given me over the years. It is an honor and a pleasure to be a part of the New Oxford World History project.

Finally, I express my deepest gratitude and love to my family—my wife, Sarah, and children, Michael and Layla—who have patiently lived with the eighteenth century and have always been helpful and supportive.

Notes

CHAPTER 1

1. J.-B. Du Halde, *A description of the empire of China and Chinese-Tartary, together with the kingdoms of Korea and Tibet: containing the geography and history (natural as well as civil) of those countries. Enriched with general and particular maps, and adorned with a great number of cuts. From the French of J. B. Du Halde, Jesuit. With Notes geographical, historical, and critical, and other improvements, particularly in the Maps, by the translator*, vol. 1 (London: T. Gardner, 1738), 232–3.

2. Quoted in Gu Huang, "The Kangxi Emperor's Changing Attitudes toward Westerners: Scientific Curiosity, Religious Toleration and Strategic Vigilance" (M.A. thesis, University of Southern California, 1995), 16.

3. Quoted in Jonathan D. Spence, *The Search for Modern China*, 2nd ed. (New York: W. W. Norton, 1999), 122.

4. Rebecca Larson, *Daughters of Light: Quaker Women Preaching and Prophesying in the Colonies and Abroad, 1700–1775* (New York: Alfred A. Knopf, 1999), 314.

5. George Fox, *The Lambs Officer is gone forth with the Lambs Message* (London: Thomas Simmons, 1659), 7, 13–14.

6. Alexander Hamilton, *A new account of the East Indies, being the observations and remarks of Capt. Alexander Hamilton, who spent his time there from the year 1688 to 1723, Trading and travelling, by sea and land…* (Edinburgh: John Mosman, 1727), 1: 147. *Eighteenth Century Collections Online*. Gale. Georgetown University. July 4, 2012.

7. The discussion of Mulla Abdul Ghafur is based on Ashin Das Gupta, *The World of the Indian Ocean Merchant, 1500–1800* (New Delhi: Oxford University Press, 2001), 95–101.

8. Daniel Defoe, *A brief state of the question between the printed and painted calicoes and the woollen and silk manufacture, as far as it relates to the wearing and using of printed and painted calicoes in Great Britain*, 3rd ed. (London, 1720). *Eighteenth Century Collections Online*. Gale. Georgetown University. August 11, 2011.

9. Quoted in Eugen Weber, *Peasants into Frenchmen* (Stanford: Stanford University Press, 1976), 117.

10. William Wordsworth, "The Excursion, Book Eighth, The Parsonage," in William Wordsworth, *The Complete Poetical Works* (London: Macmillan, 1888, online ed., 1999), www.bartleby.com/lit-hub/the-complete-works-4/contents, lines 118–21, 128–30.

11. Richard Guest, *A Compendious History of the Cotton-manufacture* (Manchester: Joseph Pratt, 1823), 47.

12. Stanislaw Poniatowski, *Remarks on M. de Voltaire's History of Charles XII, King of Sweden* (London: J. Brindley, 1741), 76–7. *Eighteenth Century Collections Online*. Gale. Georgetown University. January 7, 2012. Spelling as in the original source.

13. *The Authority of the Pope rejected by the Jesuits in China, or, A complaint of Cardinal Tournon of their disobedience* (London: John Morphew, 1708), 4. *Eighteenth Century Collections Online*. Gale. Georgetown University. July 2, 2012.

14. Madame (Marie-Catherine) d'Aulnoy, *The ingenious and diverting letters of the lay's——travels into Spain* (London: Samuel Crouch, 1708), 134. *Eighteenth Century Collections Online*. Georgetown University. July 3, 2012.

15. Penelope Aubin, *The Strange adventures of the Count de Vinevil and his family* (London: E. Bell, 1721), 69. *Eighteenth Century Collections Online*. Georgetown University. July 3, 2012.

16. Hamilton, *A new account of the East Indies*, 1:37.

17. "Letter XXVI," *Persian Letters*, in *The Complete Works of M. de Montesquieu* (Dublin: W. Watson et al., 1777), 3:264.

18. Andries Stockenström, quoted in Andy Smith et al., *The Bushmen of Southern Africa* (Athens: Ohio University Press, 2000), 42.

19. Quoted in Pierre-Etienne Will, *Bureaucracy and Famine in Eighteenth Century China*, trans. Elborg Forster (Stanford: Stanford University Press, 1990), 181.

20. Quoted in Eloise Talcott Hibbert, *Jesuit Adventure in China: During the Reign of K'ang Hsi* (New York: E. P. Dutton, 1941), 187.

21. Jonathan D. Spence, *Emperor of China: Self-portrait of K'ang-his* (New York: Random House/Vintage Books, 1988), 54.

22. Spence, *Emperor of China*, 146.

23. Spence, *Emperor of China*, 44.

24. Tony Ballantyne, "Hamilton, Alexander (b. before 1688, d. in or after 1733)", *Oxford Dictionary of National Biography* (London: Oxford University Press, 2004), https://doi-org.proxy.library.georgetown.edu/10.1093/ref.odnb/12042, accessed July 4, 2012.

25. Judasz Tadeusz Krusinki, *An Historical Account of the Revolutions in Persia* (London: J. Roberts, 1727), title page.

26. Quoted in Abderrahmane El Moudden, "The ambivalence of *rihla*: community integration and self-definition in Moroccan travel accounts, 1300–1800," in *Muslim Travellers: Pilgrimage, Migration, and the Religious Imagination*, ed. Dale F. Eickelman and James Piscatori (Berkeley: University of California Press, 1990), 79.

27. John Bowles, *Reflections on the Political and Moral State of Society at the Close of the Eighteenth Century* (London: F. and C. Rivington, 1800), 77. *Eighteenth Century Collections Online*. Gale. Georgetown University. September 8, 2016.

28. Fray Buenaventura de Salinas, *Memoria de las Historias del Nuevo Mundo*, as quoted in Antonine Tibesar, "The alternativa: a study of Spanish-Creole relations in seventeenth-century Peru," *The Americas* 11.3 (1955): 240.

CHAPTER 2

1. "Preface to the *Discourses* by Roger North," Appendix G in Tichard Grassby, *The English Gentleman in Trade: The Life and Works of Sir Dudley North, 1641–1691* (Oxford: Clarendon Press, 1994), 356.

2. Mr. (John) Oldmixon, *The British Empire in America* (London: John Nicholson, 1708), 2:343–4. *Eighteenth Century Collections Online*. Gale. Georgetown University. September 10, 2016.

3. Oldmixon, 1:xxxvii.

4. Oldmixon, 2:343.

5. *Letter Written from Constantinople by an English Lady, who was lately in Turkey, and who is no less distinguished by her Wit than by her Quality; to a Venetian Nobleman* (London: J. Roberts, 1719), 5.

6. Quoted in John K. Thornton, *The Congolese Saint Anthony: Dona Beatriz Kimpa Vita and the Antonian Movement, 1684–1706* (Cambridge: Cambridge University Press, 1998), 10.

7. Quoted in Thornton, *The Congolese Saint Anthony*, 121.

8. Quoted in Thornton, *The Congolese Saint Anthony*, 115.

9. Carl von Linné, *Iter Lapponicum*, quoted in Wilfrid Blunt, *Linnaeus: The Complete Naturalist*, reprint ed. (Princeton: Princeton University Press, 2001), 69.

10. Anders Sparrman, quoted in Andy Smith, Candy Malherbe, Mat Guenther, and Penny Berens, *The Bushmen of Southern Africa: A Foraging Society in Transition* (Athens: Ohio University Press, 2000), 29.

11. As quoted in Ronald Wright, *Stolen Continents: The Americas through Indian Eyes since 1492* (Boston: Houghton Mifflin, 1992), 116.

12. As cited in Wright, *Stolen Continents*, 116.

13. Voltaire, *Candide, ou l'Optimisme*, ch. 26.

14. William Makepeace Thackery, *The Four Georges* (Garden City, NY: Doubleday-Dolphin), 19.

15. *Maāsir-I-'Āamgiri: A History of the Emperor Aurangzib-'Āamgir (reign 1658–1707 A.D.)*, trans. Jadu-nath Sarkar (Calcutta: Royal Asiatic Society of Bengal, 1947), 312.

16. "Funeral Sermon on Peter the Great," in Leo Wiener, ed. and tr., *Anthology of Russian Literature from the Earliest Period to the Present Time* (New York: G. P. Putnam's, 1902), 1:216.

17. Dangeau, Philippe de Courcillon, Marquis de, *Mémoire sur la mort de Louis XIV* (Paris: Didot frères, 1858), 24.

18. Quoted in Philip Bobbitt, *The Shield of Achilles: War, Peace, and the Course of History* (New York: Alred A. Knopf, 2002), 129.

19. Philip D. Curtin, *Cross-Cultural Trade in World History* (Cambridge: Cambridge University Press, 1984), ch. 1.

20. Quoted in Anita McConnell, "North, Roger (1588–1652/3)," *Oxford Dictionary of National Biography* (Oxford: Oxford University Press, 2004), 41:113.

21. Eric Gilbert and Jonathan T. Reynolds, *Trading Tastes: Commodity and Culture Exchange to 1750* (Upper Saddle River, NJ: Pearson-Prentice Hall, 2006), 97.

22. William Cleland, *The present state of the sugar plantations consider'd; but more especially that of the island of Barbadoes* (London: John Morphew, 1713). *Eighteenth Century Collections Online.* Gale. Georgetown University. September 10, 2016.

23. F. W. Baller, *The Sacred Edict with a Translation of the Colloquial Rendering, Notes, and Vocabulary* (Shanghai: American Presbyterian Mission Press, 1892), 71. Google Books online.

24. Quoted in G. Creel, *Chinese Thought from Confucius to Mao Tsê-tung* (Chicago: University of Chicago Press, 1969), 225.

25. Huang Zongxi, quoted in Creel, *Chinese Thought*, 223.

26. Ahmad Sirhindi, *Maktubat*, quoted in Aziz Ahmad, *Studies in Islamic Culture in the Indian Environment* (Oxford: Clarendon Press, 1964), 183.

27. M. Cornelius Le [De] Bruyn, *Travels into Muscovy, Persia, and Part of the East-Indies* (London: A. Bettesworth and C. Hitch, et al., 1737), 1:211.

28. Le Bruyn, *Travels*, 1:211.

29. Muhammad Baqir al-Majlisi, *'Ayn al-hayat*, as quoted in Abdul-Hadi Hairi, "Madjlisi," *Encyclopaedia of Islam*, 2nd ed. (Leiden: E. J. Brill, 1985), 5:1087.

30. *Statutes of the Realm*, Vol. 7: *1695–1701*, ed. John Raithby (1820), 636–8.

31. Dogmatic Constitution issued by Pope Clement XI on September 8, 1713. *Papal Encyclicals Online.* www.papalencyclicals.net/Clem11/c11unige.htm, accessed August 1, 2008.

32. *The Pietists: Selected Writings,* ed. Emilie Griffin and Peter C. Erb (New York: HarperCollins/HarperSanFrancisco, 2006), 7.

33. William Penn, *Primitive Christianity Revived,* ch. 1, §1. Reprinted in web site of Street Corner Society. www.readex.com/products/early-american-imprints, series 1 Evans, 1639–1800.

34. Glückel, *The Memoirs of Glückel of Hameln,* trans. Marvin Lowenthal (New York: Schocken Books, 1977), 47.

35. "Thirty-Six Aphorisms of the Baal Shem Tov," http://www.chabad.org, accessed September 3, 2011.

36. *An Account of the Life and Writings of Sr Isaac Newton. Translated from the Eloge of M. Fontenelle, Secretary of the Academy of Sciences at Paris,* 2nd ed. (London: T. Warner, 1727), 9. *Eighteenth Century Collections Online.* Gale. September 8, 2016.

37. Thomas Brereton, *The Criticks, being Papers upon the Times* (London: W. Chetwood, 1719), 1:218. *Eighteenth Century Collections Online.* Gale.

38. *A Collection of Papers Which passed between the late Learned Mr. Leibnitz and Dr. Clarke in the Years 1715 and 1716* (London: James Knapton, 1717), v. *Eighteenth Century Collections Online.* Gale.

39. *The Oxford Dictionary of Quotations,* 2nd ed. (London: Oxford University Press, 1953), 382.
CHAPTER 3

1. From *A Source Book for Russian History,* trans. G. Vernadsky (New Haven: Yale University Press, 1972), vol. 2, as presented in the online *Internet History Sourcebook,* http://www.fordham.edu/halsall.

2. *Ching-Tê-Chên T'ao-Lu or The Potteries of China,* trans. Geoffrey R. Sayer (London: Routledge and Kegan Paul, 1951), 49.

3. *Ching-Tê-Chên T'ao-Lu,* 49.

4. Richard Steele, *The Lover* (London: J. Tonson, 1715), 62. *Eighteenth Century Collections Online.* Gale. September 8, 2016.

5. From the preface of *Musaffā* as translated and quoted in S. Abul A'la Maududi, *A Short History of the Revivalist Movement in Islam,* trans. Al-Ash'ari (Lahore: Islamic Publications, 1976), 100.

6. Definition as quoted from Marcia K. Hermansen, *Shah Wali Allah of Delhi's, Hujjat Allah Al-Baligha,* in Nazeem M. I. Goolam, "Ijtihad and its Significance for Legal Interpretation," *Michigan State Law Review* (2006): 1458, with analysis by Goolam.

7. Quoted in Ronald Wright, *Stolen Continents: The Americas through Indian Eyes since 1492* (Boston: Houghton Mifflin, 1992).

8. As quoted in Robert K. Massie, *Catherine the Great: Portrait of a Woman* (New York: Random House, 2011), 396.

9. J. Castéra, *History of Catharine II, Empress of Russia,* trans. Henry Hunter (London: John Stockdale, 1800), 356.

10. Quoted in Robert K. Massie, *Catherine the Great: Portrait of a Woman* (New York: Random House, 2011), 403.

11. Castéra, *History of Catharine II,* 371.
118   NOTES TO PAGES 50–60

12. The speeches were recorded by an officer present and published in [Thomas Anburey], *Travels through the Interior Parts of America in a Series of Letters by an Officer* (London: William Lane, 1789), 1:285, 289.

13. Lewis de Bougainville, *A Voyage round the World Performed by Order of His Most Christian Majesty, In the Years 1766, 1767, 1768, and 1769*, trans. John Reinhold Forster (London: J. Nourse, 1772), 252–3.

14. David Samwell, "Some Account of a Voyage to South Sea's," Appendix II, in J. C. Beaglehole, ed., *The Voyage of the Resolution and Discovery, 1776–1780* (Cambridge: Cambridge University Press, 1967), 2:1190.

15. William H. McNeill, *The Age of Gunpowder Empires, 1450–1800* (Washington, DC: American Historical Association, 1989).

16. Quoted in Mark C. Elliott, *Emperor Qianlong, Son of Heaven, Man of the World* (New York: Longman, 2009), 52.

17. W. F. Reddaway, ed., *Documents of Catherine the Great* (New York: Russell & Russell, 1971), 289.

18. Cotton Mather, *A Memorial of the Present Deplorable State of New-England* (Boston: S. Phillips et al., 1707). *Eighteenth Century Collections Online*. Gale. September 8, 2016.

19. Mather, *A Memorial*, 1.

20. Mather, *A Memorial*, 2.

21. Don Jorge Juan and Don Antonio de Ulloa, *Discourse and Political Reflections on the Kingdoms of Peru*, trans. John J. TePaske and Besse A. Clement (Norman: University of Oklahoma Press, 1978), 217.

22. *The Beauties of the Spectators, Tatlers, and Guardians, connected and digested under alphabetical heads* (London: J. & R. Tonson et al., 1753), 1:218. *Eighteenth Century Collections Online*. Gale. September 8, 2016.

23. *The Beauties of the Spectators*, 1:218, 219.

24. Pierre-Daniel Huet, *A View of the Dutch Trade in all the States, Empires, and Kingdoms in the World*, 2nd ed. (London: J. Walthoe, 1722), 141. *Eighteenth Century Collections Online*. Gale. September 8, 2016.

25. Jo. Jacob Berlu, *The Treasury of Drugs Unlocked* (London: S. Clarke, 1733), 17–18.

26. As quoted in J. E. Inikori, "The Import of Firearms into West Africa, 1750–1807: A Quantitative Analysis," *Journal of African History* 18.3 (1977): 344.

27. Harry Verelst, *A view of the rise, progress, and present state of the English government in Bengal* (London: J. Nourse, 1792), 62. *The Making of the Modern World*. Gale 2009. Gale, Cengage Learning. Gale Document Number U3601588249.

28. The Charter as quoted in Anita McConnell, "North, Roger (1588–1652/3)," *Oxford Dictionary of National Biography* (Oxford: Oxford University Press, 2004); online ed., January 2008, http://www.oxforddnb.com.proxy.library. georgetown.edu/view/article/20313.

29. *Izālat al-khafā*, 2:377, as cited in Saiyid Athar Abbas Rizvi, *Shāh Walī-Allāh and His Times* (Canberra: Ma'rifat Publishing, 1980), 262.

30. *The Conclusive Argument from God: Shāh Walī Allāh of Delhi's Hujjat Allāh al-Bāligha*, trans. Marcia K. Hermansen (Leiden: E. J. Brill, 1996), 26.

31. *The Conclusive Argument*, 4.

32. *The Conclusive Argument*, 272.

33. Quoted in Jamaal Al-Din M. Zarabozo, *The Life, Teachings, and Influence of Muhammad Ibn Abdul-Wahhab* (Riyadh: Ministry of Islamic Affairs, The Kingdom of Saudi Arabia, 2003/1427[AH]), 102.

34. Quoted in Philip S. Watson, compiler, *The Message of the Wesleys: A Reader of Instruction and Devotion* (New York: Macmillan, 1964), 29–30.

35. François Marie Arouet de Voltaire, "'He Would Have to Be Invented': to Frederick the Great, 1770," in *The Portable Age of Reason Reader*, ed. Crane Brinton (New York: Viking Press, 1956), 367.

36. Isaac Newton, *Opticks: or a Treatise of the Reflections, Refractions, Inflections and Colours of Light*, 4th ed. (London: William Innys, 1730), 344. *Eighteenth Century Collections Online*. Gale. September 8, 2016.

37. *Encyclopaedia Britannica; or a Dictionary of Arts and Sciences* (Edinburgh: A. Bell, 1771), 3:362.

38. Immanuel Kant, "An Answer to the Question: 'What is Enlightenment'," translation from https://enlightenment.commons.gc.cuny.edu/files/2016/12/Kant-what-is-Enlightenment, accessed December 21, 2009.

CHAPTER 4

1. Quoted in Deborah Valenze, *The First Industrial Woman* (New York: Oxford University Press, 1995), 87. The tombstone inscription is from Alfred P. Wadsworth and Julia De Lacy Mann, *The Cotton Trade and Industrial Lancaster, 1600–1780* (reprint, 1931. New York: Augustus M. Kelley, 1968), 492.

2. Laurent Dubois, *Avengers of the New World: The Story of the Haitian Revolution* (Cambridge, MA: Belknap Press of Harvard University Press, 2004), 40.

3. Quoted in Madison Smartt Bell, *Toussaint Louverture, A Biography* (New York: Vintage Books, 2007), 59–60.

4. A text of the full letter is in Bell, *Toussaint Louverture*, 39–41.

5. Quoted in Laurent Dubois, *Avengers*, 243.

6. The translation of the text is Document 44, "The Haitian Declaration of Independence, January 1, 1804," in Laurent Dubois and John D. Garrigus, *Slave Revolution in the Caribbean, 1789–1804: A Brief History with Documents* (New York: Bedford/St. Martin's, 2006). An analysis of the name "Haiti" is in Laurent Dubois, *Avengers*, 298–9.

7. Joseph Priestley, *The present State of Europe compared with Antient Prophecies; A Sermon Preached at the Gravel Pit Meeting in Hackney, February 28, 1794* (London: J. Johnson, 1794), 2.

8. Quoted in Hillel Schwartz, *Century's End: A Cultural History of the Fin de Siecle from the 990s through the 1990s* (New York: Doubleday, 1990), 132.

9. John Adams, *A view of universal history, from the creation to the present time* (London: G. Kearsley, 1795), 2:313–14.

10. Quoted in Thomas W. Kavanagh, *Comanche Political History: An Ethnohistorical Perspective, 1706–1875* (Lincoln: University of Nebraska Press, 1996), 102, 163.

11. L. E. Threlkeld, as quoted in Niel Gunson, "Pomare II of Tahiti and Polynesian Imperialism," *Journal of Pacific History* 4 (1969): 68.

12. Neville Wyndham, *Travels through Europe* (London: M. D. Symonds, [1790]), 3:411, 414. *Eighteenth Century Collections Online*. Gale. September 8, 2016.

13. Quoted in Linda Cooke Johnson, *Shanghai: From Market Town to Treaty Port, 1074–1858* (Stanford: Stanford University Press, 1995), 160.

14. Tobias Lear to James Madison, Secretary of State, July 17, 1801. US National Archives and Records, Record Group 59, Miscellaneous Letters, cited in www.pbs.org/wgbh/aia/part3/3h491t.html.

15. Thomas Paine, *Common Sense*, "New edition, with several additions to the body of the work" (Philadelphia: W. & T. Bradford, 1791), 89–90. *Eighteenth Century Collections Online*. Gale.

16. Preamble, The Constitution of the Commonwealth of Massachusetts, from the General Court of the Commonwealth of Massachusetts, http://malegislature.gov/laws/comstitution.

17. Thomas Jefferson, "Letter to Judge Spencer Roane," September 6, 1819.

18. Quoted in James B. Collins, *The Ancien Régime and the French Revolution* (Toronto: Wadsworth, 2002), 55.

19. "The Tennis Court Oath (June 20, 1789)" *The French Revolution: A Document Collection* New York: Houghton Mifflin, 1999), 60–1.

20. Quoted in Georget Dutton, *The Tây Son Uprising* (Honolulu: University of Hawai'i Press, 2006), 82.

21. Uthman Ibn Fudi, *Bayan wujub al-hijra 'ala 'l-'ibad*, trans. F. H. El Masri (Khartoum: Khartoum University Press, 1978), 51.

22. Quoted in Ward Stavig, *The World of Túpac Amaru* (Lincoln: University of Nebraska Press, 1999), 242.

23. Quoted in Stavig, *The World of Túpac Amaru*, 239.

24. *Memoirs of Prince Metternich, 1773–1815*, ed. Prince Richard Metternich (New York: Charles Scribner's Sons, 1881), 2:355.

25. "Bhagwan Swaminarayan: Teenage Yogi," http://www.swaminarayan.org/lordswaminarayan/biography/2.htm.

26. Raymond Brady Williams, *An Introduction to Swaminarayan Hinduism* (Cambridge: Cambridge University Press, 2001), 2 and 17.

27. John Wesley, *Thoughts upon Slavery* (London: Joseph Crukshank; reprinted in Philadelphia, 1778), 52–3. Electronic edition in University of North Carolina at Chapel Hill digitization project, *Documenting the American South*.

28. Quoted in Eric Metaxas, *Amazing Grace: William Wilberforce and the Heroic Campaign to End Slavery* (San Francisco: HarperSanFrancisco, 2007), 85.

29. William Wilberforce, *A Practical View of the Prevailing Religious System of Professed Christians in the Higher and Middle Classes in this Country Contrasted with Real Christianity* (Boston: Crocker & Brewster, 1829), 78 and 80.

30. *A Parliamentary History of England from the Earliest Period to the year 1803* (London: T. C. Hansard, 1817), 29:278.

31. Charles Tilly and Lesley J. Wood, *Social Movements, 1768–2008*, 2nd ed. (Boulder: Paradigm Publishers, 2009), 33.

32. Quoted in Robert N. Bellah, *Tokugawa Religion* (Glencoe: The Free Press, 1957), 100.

33. Quoted in Bellah, *Tokugawa Religion*, 101. Italics added.

34. Quoted in Barbara Daly Metcalf, *Islamic Revival in British India: Deoband, 1860–1900* (Princeton: Princeton University Press, 1982), 46.

35. Shah Ismail, as quoted in Aziz Ahmad, *Studies in Islamic Culture in the Indian Environment* (Oxford: Clarendon Press, 1964), 213.

36. Quoted in R. R. Palmer, "Notes on the Use of the Word 'Democracy' 1789–1799," *Political Science Quarterly* 68.2 (1953): 221.

37. Thomas O'Bien Hanley, ed., *The John Carroll Papers* (Notre Dame: University of Notre Dame Press, 1976), 1:80–1.

38. Joseph Priestley, *Experiments and Observations on Different Kinds of Air*, 2nd ed. (London: J. Johnson, 1775), xii.

39. See the discussion of this aspect of Priestley in Robert E. Schofield, *The Enlightened Joseph Priestley* (University Park: Pennsylvania State University Press, 2004), xiii and passim.

40. Priestley, *Experiments*, x.

41. [Guyton] de Morveau, [Antoine] Lavoisier, [Claude Louis] Berthollet, and [Antoine] de Fourcroy, *Méthode de Nomenclature Chimique* (Paris, 1787).

42. Quoted in Herbert Butterfield, *The Origins of Modern Science*, rev. ed. (New York: Free Press, 1957), 217.

43. Arnold Toynbee, *Lectures on the Industrial Revolution of the Eighteenth Century in England*, reprinted new ed. (London: Longmans Green, 1912), 204.

44. "Cotton," *Encyclopædia Britannica or a Dictionary of Arts and Sciences* (Edinburgh: A. Bell and C. Macfarquhar, 1771), 2:284.

45. Quoted in Clare Le Corbeiller and Alice Cooney Frelinghuysen, "Chinese Export Porcelain," *Metropolitan Museum of Art Bulletin*, new series, 60.3 (2003): 34.

EPILOGUE

1. Quoted in Jonathan D. Spence, *The Search for Modern China*, 2nd ed. (New York: W. W. Norton, 1999), 122.

2. George Staunton, *An Authentic Account of an Embassy from the King of Great Britain to the Emperor of China* (Philadelphia: Robert Campbell, 1799), I:2.

3. Quoted in Spence, *The Search for Modern China*, 123.

4. Quoted in Marla R. Miller, *Betsy Ross and the Making of America* (New York: Henry Holt, 2010), 238.

5. Quoted in the analysis of this process in Sven Beckert, *Empire of Cotton: A Global History* (New York: Alfred A. Knopf, 2014), 43–4.

6. R. Brookes, *The General Gazetteer or Compendius Dictionary*, 11th ed. (London, 1800), 637. *Eighteenth Century Collections Online*. Gale.

7. J. M. Campbell, ed., *Gazetteer of the Bombay Presidency: Gujarat: Surat and Broach*, vol. II (Bombay: Government Central Press, 1877; reprinted: Charleston, SC: Nabu Press, 2010), 110.

8. John Bowles, *Reflections on the Political and Moral State of Society at the Close of the Eighteenth Century* (London: F. and C. Rivington, 1800), 122.

9. William Linn, "A Funeral Eulogy on General Washington," in *Eulogies and Orations on the Life and Death of General George Washington, First President of the United States of America* (Boston: Manning and Loring, 1800), 172–3.

Further Reading

CHAPTER 1: THE WORLD OF 1700: CONTINUITY AND CHANGE

Harris, Ron. *Going the Distance: Eurasian Trade and the Rise of the Business Corporation, 1400–1700*. Princeton: Princeton University Press, 2020.

Larson, Rebecca, *Daughters of Light: Quaker Women Preaching and Prophesying in the Colonies and Abroad, 1700–1775*. New York: Alfred A. Knopf, 1999.

McNeill, William H. *The Age of Gunpowder Empires 1450–1800*. Washington, DC: American Historical Association, 1989.

Spence, Jonathan D. *Emperor of China: Self-portrait of K'ang-hsi*. New York: Random House/Vintage, 1988.

Wright, Ronald. *Stolen Continents: The Americas through Indian Eyes Since 1492*. Boston: Houghton Mifflin, 1992.

CHAPTER 2: CLIMAXES AND NEW BEGINNINGS

Gilbert, Eric, and Jonathan T. Reynolds. *Trading Tastes: Commodity and Culture Exchange to 1750*. Upper Saddle River, NJ: Pearson, 2005.

Marks, Robert B. *The Origins of the Modern World: A Global and Ecological Narrative*. 5th ed. Lanham, MD: Rowman and Littlefield, 2024.

Sajdi, Dana, ed. *Ottoman Tulips, Ottoman Coffee: Leisure and Lifestyle in the Eighteenth Century*. London: I. B. Taurus, 2014.

Thornton, John K. *The Kongolese Saint Anthony: Dona Beatriz Kimpa Vita and the Antonian Movement 1684–1706*. Cambridge: Cambridge University Press, 1998.

Westfall, Richard S. *Isaac Newton*. Oxford: Oxford University Press, 2007.

CHAPTER 3: MONARCHS, TRADE COMPANIES, AND REVIVALISTS

Curtin, Philip. *The Rise and Fall of the Plantation Complex*. 2nd ed. Cambridge: Cambridge University Press, 1998.

Ferrone, Vincentze, *The World of the Enlightenment*. Trans. Elisabetta Taranteno and Martin Mclaughlin. London: Routledge, 2025.

Garretsen, Anne. *The City of Blue and White: Chinese Porcelain and the Early Modern World*. Cambridge: Cambridge University Press, 2020.

Massie, Robert K. *Catherine the Great: Portrait of a Woman*. New York: Random House, 2011.

Rizvi, Saiyid Athar Abbas. *Shah Wali Allah and his Times*. Canberra: Ma'rifat Publishing, 1980.

CHAPTER 4: SHIFTING BALANCES AND REVOLUTIONS

Beckert, Sven. *Empire of Cotton: A Global History*. New York: Alfred A. Knopf, 2014.

Dubois, Laurent. *Avengers of the New World: The Story of the Haitian Revolution*. Cambridge, MA: Belknap Press, 2004.

Johnson, Linda Cooke. *Shanghai: From Market Town to Treaty Port, 1074–1858*. Stanford: Stanford University Press, 1995.

Kavanaugh, Thomas W. *Comanche Political History: An Ethnohistorical Perspective*. Lincoln: University of Nebraska Press, 1996.

Valenze, Deborah. *The First Industrial Woman*. New York: Oxford University Press, 1995.
EPILOGUE: THE WORLD IN THE EIGHTEENTH CENTURY

Bayly, C. A. *The Birth of the Modern World 1780–1914*. Oxford: Blackwell, 2004.

Elliott, Mark C. *Emperor Qianlong: Son of Heaven, Man of the World*. New York: Longman, 2009.

Miller, Marla R. *Betsy Ross and the Making of America*. New York: Henry Holt, 2010.

Pomeranz, Kenneth, *The Great Divergence: China, Europe, and the Making of the Modern World Economy*. Princeton: Princeton University Press, 2000.
124   FURTHER READING

Index

CHRONOLOGICAL VOLUMES
The World from Beginnings to 4000 BCE
The World from 4000 to 1000 BCE
The World from 1000 BCE to 300 CE
The World from 300 to 1000 CE
The World from 1000 to 1500
The World from 1450 to 1700
The Twentieth Century: A World History

THEMATIC AND TOPICAL VOLUMES
The City: A World History
Democracy: A World History
Empires: A World History
Food: A World History
The Family: A World History
Gender: A World History
Genocide: A World History
Health and Medicine: A World History
Migration: A World History
Race: A World History
Technology: A World History

GEOGRAPHICAL VOLUMES
The Atlantic in World History
The Balkans in World History
Central Asia in World History
China in World History
The Indian Ocean in World History
Iran in World History
Japan in World History
Mexico in World History
Russia in World History
The Silk Road in World History
South Africa in World History
South Asia in World History
Southeast Asia in World History
Trans-Saharan Africa in World History